Reflection & Controversy

R

Reflection & Controversy

Essays on Social Work

Ann Hartman

NASW PRESS

Ann A. Abbott, PhD, ACSW, President
Sheldon R. Goldstein, ACSW, LISW, Executive Director

National Association of Social Workers • Washington, DC

                                                    r
                                            of Editorial Services
                                           tor

Robert Elwood, Indexer
Elizabeth Mitchell, Proofreader

Cover and text designed by Bagnell & Socha, Philadelphia, PA
Text composed by Bagnell & Socha, Philadelphia, PA
Cover photograph by Paul Barton Photography, New York, NY
Type set in Bembo and printed on Springhill
Printed and bound by Boyd Printing Company, Albany, NY

©1994 by the NASW Press

Library of Congress Cataloging-in-Publication Data

Hartman, Ann.
      Reflection & controversy : essays on social work /
  Ann Hartman.
      p. cm.
      Includes bibliographical references and index.
      ISBN 0-87101-233-2 (pbk.)
      1. Social service. 2. Social service—United States.
  3. Social policy. 4. United States—Social policy.
  I. Title.   II. Title: Reflection and controversy
      HV37.H37 1994
      361.973—dc20

                                    93–44231
                                        CIP

Printed in the United States of America.

Contents

Foreword   vii
    Carel B. Germain

Preface   ix
    Linda Beebe

Introduction
    Changing of the Guard   3

Many Ways of Knowing
    Many Ways of Knowing   11
    Enriching Our Profession's Narrative   17
    In Search of Subjugated Knowledge   23

Equity and Justice
    Aging Is a Feminist Issue   31
    Words Create Worlds   37
    It Was Not Our Finest Hour   43
    A Message from Los Angeles   49
    Out of the Closet: Revolution and Backlash   55

The World
    Our Global Village   65
    War Stories   71

The Nation
    Good Luck, Bill—Keep in Touch   79
    Writing a New Story about America   85

Social Policy
    Homelessness: Public Issue and Private Trouble   91
    Where Do We Go from Here?   97
        Caitlin C. Ryan
    Toward a Redefinition and Recontextualization   103
        of the Abortion Issue
    Health Care: Privilege or Entitlement?   109

Families and Children
    Children in a Careless Society   117
    Violence and Families   123
        Liane V. Davis
    Family Ties   131
    Murphy Brown, Dan Quayle, and the   137
        American Family
    Family Preservation under Attack   143

The Profession
    Still between Client and Community   153
    A Profession Chasing Its Tail—Again   159
    Social Worker-in-Situation   165
    The Professional Is Political   171

Index   179

Foreword

This collection of editorials beckons us toward the new millennium and all that lies ahead for the social work profession and for the many populations in diverse environments whom we serve. Appearing in *Social Work* from September 1989 to December 1993, these editorials were written by Ann Hartman, editor-in-chief, and two invited experts. Like many readers of *Social Work*, I savored each editorial as it appeared; each was a learning experience in professional excellence. But rereading them now as a coherent whole is an inspiring experience that engenders new pride in and hope for the profession. I now view the collection not as bimonthly editorials, but as highly significant essays that will guide seasoned social work practitioners, students, and educators to excellence-in-action in the times ahead.

The deeply disturbing, sadly painful, but accurate analysis of professional and societal issues in these essays arises from Hartman's love of country and her lifelong devotion to social work. Her conviction is that both America and social work can and will do better. Thus each essay is wrapped lovingly in the mantle of caring, whether the topic is direct services to individuals, families, groups, neighborhoods, and communities; issues of varied types of knowledge and research; social policy and program development; or advocacy and action for social change.

To the reader's benefit, Hartman possesses a rare ability to intelligently present and analyze important ideas within a very limited space and to make them rousing as well. Her analyses of issues are consistently well balanced, especially important for controversial issues. For example, the essay on pro-life and pro-choice issues in abortion carefully analyzes positive and negative positions assumed by both. In contrast, the reflective essays stimulate and refresh the reader's own reflections.

The commitment of contemporary social work to empower oppressed and vulnerable populations is addressed in several essays that also clarify the characteristics of a truly empowering stance for the profession. Historically, empowerment was first articulated by Jane Addams and first enacted by Bertha Capen Reynolds. And now we are challenged as individuals to examine our professional conscience to see how far we are personally committed to such a stance.

Hartman offers fresh insight into long-standing professional polarities that divide us today as they did historically. The dialectics include such antithetical commitments as private troubles and public issues, residual and institutional perspectives on services and programs, cause and function (social reform and direct service), and generic and specific approaches to practice and to the nature of knowledge itself. More importantly, the essays offer sensitive and sensible agendas for melding what needs to be melded to make the profession whole again.

All Americans, not only social workers and other human services professionals, should be reading and discussing these remarkable essays. The essays cover a wide range of issues from homelessness to political correctness, from children in a careless society to aging as a feminist issue, from health care to war and peace, from narrative theory to revolution and backlash in our gay and lesbian communities. Singularly and together, the essays represent a fearless and eloquent voice addressing the major interconnected societal, global, and professional traumas of our time, of time past, and of time future. Each essay illuminates a pathway to potential resolution for all Americans to consider.

Carel B. Germain

Carel B. Germain, DSW, is emerita professor, University of Connecticut School of Social Work, West Hartford, CT. Following practice experience in child welfare, child guidance, and health and mental health, Dr. Germain was professor of social work at the University of Maryland, Columbia University, and the University of Connecticut, where she also served as acting dean. Dr. Germain has provided practice seminars in the United States, Canada, Sweden, and Great Britain.

Preface

Staff and volunteers for the NASW Press are very pleased to offer this rich collection of Ann Hartman's essays on social work. Over the past $4^1/_2$ years, we—like Carel Germain and more than 100,000 readers—have savored each editorial, every one a vivid demonstration of compelling insight and humanity.

As publisher of *Social Work*, the NASW Press has received many, many letters from readers who wrote to thank Hartman for speaking to their needs or providing the knowledge that helped them in their work. We published only a few, using those that added still more to the information or those that carried the debate further. Not all the letters were favorable, of course. As the book's title indicates, some of these essays were controversial in that they probed areas of bias that many people are unwilling or unable to accept. The vituperativeness of some responses to such essays as "Not Our Finest Hour" or "Out of the Closet" was dismaying, but many respondents accepted Hartman's intellectual challenges and engaged in a higher form of dialogue than professional journals often obtain.

We also discovered over the years that professors were assigning the essays as required reading in schools of social work. Our permissions requests increased after every issue. When we began to receive responses to editorials that had been assigned as classwork, the letters reinforced our belief that a collection of the essays would be a valuable text for introductory courses. I can think of no better way to help students understand the core of the profession than to offer them this array of eloquent essays.

For the experienced practitioner, the essays encourage and challenge. Hartman reminds her readers why they became social workers and challenges them to do even more to help people deal with the world's problems.

We hope that this volume will be used by educators, by students, and by practitioners for many years.

Linda Beebe
Executive Editor

Introduction

Changing of the Guard

⁂

For 4½ years, I have had the privilege of editing this journal and of participating in an ongoing conversation with its readers. This conversation has taken place in a social, economic, and political context of change and challenge, of tragedy and hope. As I come to the end of my watch, I find myself reflecting on these years and on the events that marked them, that found their way to the pages of this journal, and that are shaping our future.

On the international level, we have been through a brief and tragic war. The face of the globe has radically changed with the dismantling of the Soviet Union and with shifts of power and realignments in Africa, Latin America, the Middle East, and Asia. Who would have believed even one year ago that this nation would witness Yitzhak Rabin and Yasir Arafat shaking hands over an agreement that may be the first step to a lasting peace in the Middle East? Who could have predicted that one by one the former Soviet Republics would separate from the Union and that ancient hostilities and rivalries would emerge in an overwhelming tide of bloodshed and suffering?

On the national level, in this brief period, President George Bush has come and gone, and a new young administration has moved into Washington, faced with enormous political, social, and economic challenges but generating high expectations and their companion, disappointment. And during this period, the nation has floundered in a seemingly intractable recession as unemployment, violence, substance abuse, homelessness, and widespread poverty have grown and solutions seem beyond our reach.

At the same time, social issues have divided America and appear to be unreconcilable. These issues run deep in American consciousness and challenge some of our most cherished values and our image of ourselves as a nation. They include issues around the rights of oppressed minorities and women, the unconscionable and growing gap between the rich and the poor, the neglect of our nation's children, and the changing definitions of the American family. These issues have risen to the surface and been enacted in dramatic ways: the Los Angeles riots, the Hill–Thomas confrontation, the violent attacks on abortion clinics, the painful struggle over gays in the military, the arguments during the presidential campaign over the definition of the American family.

And what of our profession? How has social work fared in this confusing, changing, and demanding context? We survived a 12-year period in which social programs were radically curtailed or abolished, our voices were excluded from the decision-making process, and our contributions were viewed with suspicion or contempt. But interestingly, in the past four years, as we came to the end of the "me" decade, concerns about our unraveling social fabric began to be heard, and more and more young people and those seeking a career change began to apply for admission to schools of social work. In the November 1992 election, on the national, state, and local levels, socially committed candidates for office supported by the National Association of Social Workers (NASW) were successful, and hopes for a new social and economic agenda began to grow. Once again, people in leadership positions were interested in what social workers had to say.

At the same time, the practice of the large number of social workers in health or mental health delivery systems and in private practice began to be challenged by managed care initiatives and the expanding control exerted by third-party payers. Social workers began to face a dramatic threat to their always fragile professional autonomy. The fate of this autonomy and of our place in the delivery of health and mental health services will be determined by the decisions made as the nation embarks on health care reform.

This has been the context in which this journal has been produced over the past 4½ years. We have attempted to send you a publication that relates to the issues facing social workers as professionals and as citizens of the country and the world. In my position as editor, I have been guided by several principles that have increasingly molded the journal's character. First, I believe that there are many ways of knowing—many different voices— and that those preparing this professional journal published for NASW should honor multiple epistemological positions and listen to many voices.

Second, aware of the power invested in the gatekeepers to professional knowledge, we have attempted to use that power to include rather than to exclude. We have searched for subjugated knowledge, for understandings and experiences of people who have been silenced or discredited. We have been particularly interested in learning from social work clients and have valued work that brings us their voices, that describes the nature of the immediate experience of social work practice, that portrays the encounter between practitioner and clients.

Third, we have tried to make the journal "reader friendly"—to make sure it is written in understandable language, that it does not demand highly specialized technical knowledge to be understood, and that it is alive and interesting. At the same time, our editorial staff has altered text as little as possible to preserve the variety of voices and expressive styles that our authors present.

Finally, we have tried to include articles that cover the broad range of interests, activities, and concerns of social workers.

Many people participate in the production of the journal, and if we have succeeded in at least partially achieving our goals, it is to them the credit goes: the authors who send us their work, the editorial board members and the consulting editors who review hundreds of submissions with a great deal of thought and care, and the talented and hard-working staff of the NASW editorial office. All of them, working collaboratively, make this journal possible. We owe them our thanks.

When I accepted this appointment, I knew I would be reviewing hundreds of manuscripts, and I have read all of the work of my fellow professionals with great interest. I cannot think of a better way of being in touch with what is happening in our profession. I knew I would enjoy this task, and I have.

I did not, however, really understand what it would mean to write an editorial every two months, to involve myself in this ongoing conversation with my fellow social workers. It has been an enormous challenge to tackle the major issues of the day and to speak to the readership in a way that was informative and would stimulate thought and discussion. I did not anticipate that the task would become a major preoccupation for $4^1/_2$ years, a preoccupation that has been both demanding and rewarding. The most rewarding part of it has been the dialogue, which does go both ways. I have welcomed letters in response to the editorials, some of which have been sharply critical, some enthusiastically agreeing, some adding fascinating and useful points, and some simply telling a moving personal story that a reader wanted to share. I have read every letter, and we have published as many as space would allow. I have been able to answer many personally and want to thank everyone who took the time to write. But the response has not only been by letter. Wherever I go around the country, social workers come up to me and begin to talk about a subject as though we were in the middle of an ongoing dialogue, as though we were just discussing an issue and had been inter- rupted. I have learned a great deal through this conversation with my beloved "unloved profession." It has been a wonderful expe- rience.

Occasionally people have been critical, in person or in writing, because I have not presented "both sides" of an issue. That is true. I have expressed my own opinions, often with some passion. And that is the privilege of editorship, to speak one's mind on the editorial page. But I do not speak for the profession; I do not speak for the association. No editor would be free to tackle an issue with enthusiasm and candor if she or he was con- strained by the demand to be evenhanded or representative.

And now, as it should be, we will have a new editor, with different views, a different vision of the journal and of the profession. Patricia Ewalt, Dean of the School of Social Work at the University of Hawaii and distinguished social work practi- tioner, scholar, and educator, will begin her watch on January 1, 1994. NASW President Ann Abbott is to be congratulated on her choice. Pat will bring to the journal her thoughtfulness, her extensive experience, her wisdom, and her conscientiousness. She will also bring a very special commitment to multiculturalism. She will be a wonderful editor.

I was moved and honored that the staff and volunteers of NASW Press decided to publish this collection of editorials in a single volume. I hope the collection is useful to social work practitioners and educators and particularly to students as they begin to struggle with the many issues facing the profession and the nation. I am also delighted to include two guest editorials—one by Caitlin Ryan and one by Liane Davis—that appeared during my tenure as editor of *Social Work*. They add immeasurably to the volume.

I hope these essays will be a part of an ongoing discussion of all of these issues and that, through open and active dialogue, both the profession and the nation can move to new and more sensitive, inclusive, and sophisticated levels of conversation and resolution.

First published November 1993

Many Ways of
Knowing

Many Ways of Knowing

Ⓜ

In the past decade, many of us have followed a vigorous debate in the social work literature on the nature of research and on the utility and appropriateness for the profession of different research methodologies. At times reasoned, often passionate, sometimes even abusive, this ongoing discussion raises much more than methodological issues. It brings to the surface the major epistemological, ontological, and value questions that are a continuous challenge in any human enterprise, in any practice, and certainly in any search for knowledge. The questions are explicitly or implicitly asked: What is truth? How may we know it? Or, even, is there such a thing as truth and may we ever know it?

The newest phase of this ancient dialogue began with the increasing demand for empirical testing and validation of our knowledge and practice, perhaps enunciated most precisely by Walter Hudson's (1978) famous and often-quoted axioms of treatment: "If you cannot measure the client's problem, it does not exist" and, furthermore, "If you cannot measure the client's problem, you cannot treat it" (p. 65). Around the same time, other writers were questioning the usefulness of models from the natural sciences in knowledge building for the social work profession. Joseph Vigilante (1974) asked, "Is Proof Truth?" in a profession where truths are so deeply value based, and Dennis Saleebey (1979) discussed the tension between research and practice. The debate was joined by Martha Heineman's (1981) challenge to what she termed "the obsolete scientific imperative in social work research" (p. 371).

The discussion has continued and expanded with contributions from Fischer (1981), Rein and White (1981), Schuerman (1982), Gordon (1983), Imre (1984), Haworth (1984), Mullen (1985), Weick (1987), and Peile (1988), among many others.

We are not alone in this struggle. Intellectual leaders in the sciences and the social sciences, as well as in the other helping professions, are asking the same questions and challenging each other over similar issues. The discussions have spawned a new set of "isms": constructivism, deconstructionism, modernism, postmodernism, and even feminist postmodernism, which join the more familiar "isms" often rediscussed and evaluated: pragmatism, utilitarianism, relativism, positivism, and empiricism.

Why should a journal editor and editorial board members concern themselves with these demanding, abstract, and highly theoretical discussions?

Many years ago, sociologist Florian Znaniecki (1965), in his classic study *The Social Role of the Man of Knowledge*, explored the social processes involved in the definitions of knowledge and in the boundary-maintenance and gatekeeping functions of those "men"—and now, hopefully, women too—who select materials for publication and presentation. More recently, in our own profession, H. J. Karger (1983), in a provocative analysis, reminded us that at the heart of the debate about research and the nature of knowledge is a struggle for "the political control of the direction, leadership, and the future of the profession" (p. 202). He wrote,

> Those who define the questions to be asked define the parameters of the answers, and it is the parameters of the questions and the ensuing answers that function as the lens by which people view reality. (p. 203)

In Znaniecki's tradition, Karger (1983) pointed out that

> dialogue and debate are allowed within certain parameters, with the ultimate referee being the means of communication—the social work journals. It is precisely the boundaries determined by the journals— which if not totally controlled, are at least seriously influenced by the academicians—which also limit the boundaries of the debate. (p. 204)

It is thus that every time an article is accepted or rejected, the editors make an epistemological decision that not only is part of the process of defining the profession and its truth but also has political implications in the distribution of intellectual leadership, power, and status and, in these days of "publish or perish," implications for the careers and even the incomes (Kirk & Corcoran, 1989) of academicians. Furthermore, the norms of the journals can even shape the direction of inquiry because their past acceptances suggest to aspiring explorers the kinds of explorations that will most likely appear in print.

The editorial board and the editor of this journal assume this responsibility with seriousness and humility. We are aware that each of us has an epistemological position, either implicit or explicit, that guides our selection process, shapes the journal, and thus contributes to the definition of the profession and its truths and to the distribution of status and power. It is important for these epistemological convictions to be made as explicit as possible.

This editor takes the position that there are many truths and there are many ways of knowing. Each discovery contributes to our knowledge, and each way of knowing deepens our understanding and adds another dimension to our view of the world.

We need large-scale studies in which variables can be reduced to measurable units and the results translated into the language of statistical significance. We need in-depth "thick descriptions," grounded in context, of a single case, a single instance, or even a brief exchange. For example, large-scale studies of trends in marriage today furnish helpful information about a rapidly changing social institution. But getting inside one marriage, as in the play *Who's Afraid of Virginia Wolfe?* richly displays the complexities of one marriage, leading us to new insights about the pain, the joys, the expectations, the disappointments, the intimacy, and the ultimate aloneness in relationships. Both the scientific and the artistic methods provide us with ways of knowing. And, in fact, as Clifford Geertz (1983) has pointed out, innovative thinkers in many fields are blurring the genres, finding art in science and science in art, and social theory in all human creation and activity.

There are indeed many ways of knowing and many kinds of knowers: researchers, practitioners, clients. Some seekers of truth may take a path that demands distance and objectivity, whereas others rely on deeply personal and empathic knowing. Some will find the validation of their findings through statistical analysis and probability tests. Others will find it through the intensity and authenticity of "being there" (Geertz, 1988) or through public and shared consensus in what has been called "practice wisdom" (Siporin, 1989). Some truth seekers strive to predict, whereas others turn to the past for an enhanced understanding of the present.

We must not turn our backs on any opportunities to enhance our knowledge, whether they be examinations of correlations or explications of myths, which, according to Rein and White (1981), align "rational action with normative ideals and historical commitments" (p. 16). We must attend to the theoretical advances of our scholars and academicians but also gather and listen to the "stories that rise up out of practice," which "confront, challenge, confirm, or deny the stories that 'come down' from the distal citadels of the profession" (p. 19). All of these sources are essential to our profession and should enrich the pages of this journal.

We welcome survey research, large-scale studies that discover trends and identify needs. We welcome program evaluations so that we can know more about what seems to "work." We need outcome studies, which may call upon a range of ways of knowing through a single case study, experimental designs, or longitudinal reviews that reflect upon the consequences of events or conditions or interventions. We welcome phenomenological studies that lead the explorer on uncharted paths, naturalistic and ethnographic studies that are familiar but more-disciplined extensions of the practitioner's case study (Rodwell, 1987). We are interested in heuristic approaches, in which the goal is utility rather than certainty, as well as hermeneutical and interpretive investigations, which lead us to decipher the meaning of events to clients, to significant others, and to ourselves (Scott, 1989).

We can enhance our understanding by listening to and reporting the narratives, the stories that make order and sense of human experience and "organize it into temporarily meaningful episodes" (Polkinghorne, 1988, p. 7). We can attend to the myths that link value and action, and we must respect the tacit knowledge and practice wisdom that is "inductively derived from experience, and shapes the practitioner's cognitive schema" (Scott, 1989, p. 40).

But as we open ourselves to exploring and receiving many ways of knowing, we must be ever aware that each is grounded in, and an expression of, certain ontological, epistemological, and value assumptions. These assumptions must be made explicit, because knowledge and truths can be understood and evaluated only in the context of the framing assumptions. Theories can both illuminate and obscure our vision (Scott, 1989, p. 48). They also "constitute moral intervention in the social life whose conditions of existence they seek to clarify" (Giddens, 1976, p. 8).

The boundaries of our profession are wide and deep. We are concerned about the nature of our society, about social policy, social justice, and social programs. We are concerned about human associations, about communities, neighborhoods, organizations, and families. We are concerned about the life stories and the inner experiences of the people we serve and about the meaning to them of their experiences. No one way of knowing can explore this vast and varied territory.

References

Fischer, J. (1981). The social work revolution. *Social Work, 26,* 199–207.

Geertz, C. (1983). Blurred genres: The refiguration of social thought. In *Local knowledge: Further essays in interpretive anthropology.* New York: Basic Books.

Geertz, C. (1988). *Works and lives.* Stanford, CA: Stanford University Press.

Giddens, A. (1976). *New rules of sociological method.* London: Hutchinson.

Gordon, W. E. (1983). Social work revolution or evolution? *Social Work, 28,* 181–185.

Haworth, G. D. (1984). Social work research: Practice and paradigms. *Social Service Review, 58,* 343–357.

Heineman, M. B. (1981). The absolute scientific imperative in social work research. *Social Service Review, 55,* 371–397.

Hudson, W. W. (1978). First axioms of treatment. *Social Work, 23,* 65–66.

Imre, R. W. (1984). The nature of knowledge in social work. *Social Work, 29*, 41–45.

Karger, H. J. (1983). Science, research, and social work: Who controls the profession? *Social Work, 28*, 200–205.

Kirk, S. A., & Corcoran, K. J. (1989). The $12,000 question: Does it pay to publish? *Social Work, 34*, 379–381.

Mullen, E. (1985). Methodological dilemmas in social work research. *Social Work Research & Abstracts, 21*, 12–20.

Peile, C. (1988). Research paradigms in social work: From stalemate to creative synthesis. *Social Service Review, 62*, 1–19.

Polkinghorne, D. E. (1988). *Narrative knowing and the human sciences*. Albany: State University of New York Press.

Rein, M., & White, S. H. (1981). Knowledge for practice. *Social Service Review, 55*, 1–41.

Rodwell, M. K. (1987). Naturalistic inquiry: An alternative model for social work assessment. *Social Service Review, 61*, 231–246.

Saleebey, D. (1979). The tension between research and practice: Assumptions of the experimental paradigm. *Clinical Social Work Journal, 7*, 267–284.

Schuerman, J. R. (1982). The obsolete scientific imperative in social work research. *Social Service Review, 56*, 144–148.

Scott, D. (1989). Meaning construction and social work practice. *Social Service Review, 63*, 39–51.

Siporin, M. (1989). Metamodels, models, and basics: An essay review. *Social Service Review, 63*, 474–480.

Vigilante, J. (1974). Between values and science: Education for the profession during a moral crisis or, is proof truth? *Journal of Education for Social Work, 10*, 107–115.

Weick, A. (1987). Reconceptualizing the philosophical perspective of social work. *Social Service Review, 61*, 218–230.

Znaniecki, F. (1965). *The social role of the man of knowledge*. New York: Harper & Row.

First published January 1990

Enriching Our Profession's Narrative

T his issue of *Social Work* [March 1992], as do most issues, bears witness to the breadth and variety of our profession, the multiple roles we play, the vast array of populations we serve, and the different problems we face in our daily work lives.

Three of this month's articles also challenge us to enrich our vision and to add new dimensions to our psychosocial perspective. We are asked to reach for a more complete and more holistic view of our clients, ourselves, and our world, and to expand our professional discourse and enrich the narrative of social work.

First, in an Op-Ed commentary, Carlton Cornett [pp. 101–102] asks us to attend to the spirit and to consider our clients' spiritual and religious lives when we try to understand and help them. According to the author, attention to spiritual issues encompasses concern with the meaning of life, time, immortality or mortality, and the possibility of the existence of a higher power. Because these issues are crucial elements in the lives of our clients and their beliefs about themselves and the world, the author believes we impoverish our thinking and our practice if we turn our backs on these concerns.

Cornett reminds us of our deep and strong resistance to moving into this area. It is hard for the social work profession to comfortably include issues of the spirit, not only because of our love affair with science and our concern about self-determination, but probably also because of our wish to totally separate ourselves from our early professional roots in religiously inspired noblesse oblige, in tract societies, and in other charitable organizations that offered bread with one hand and reform and religious exhortation with the other. In our retreat from our ancient heritage, we can well ask, "Have we cut ourselves off from a rich vein of human experience?" As for our wish not to take a position, avoiding and ignoring is also a position. As Gregory Bateson (1972) has taught us, we cannot *not* communicate. How do our clients interpret our silence?

Dennis Saleebey, in his article entitled "Biology's Challenge to Social Work: Embodying the Person/Environment Perspective," [pp. 112–118] takes the position that although the social work profession gives lip service to biology, theory and practice have really been disembodied. He urges us to listen to the wisdom of the body and argues that if social workers are to

> enable client resources and strengths and provide client autonomy and liberation, they must be aware of and talk about such body issues as well-being and illness, body images, death and dying, care of the body, facilitating body awareness and energies, using the body in relationships and adaptation, understanding the meaning and consequences of organismic vulnerabilities, and gaining aegis over one's own body.

He urges social workers not to become part of the metaphors of oppression through the denial of bodiliness. He also suggests that "Professional artistry, the availability of tacit knowledge, and a genuinely reflective practice all may require bodily awareness and bodily presence on the part of the practitioner."

Various resistances also block our ability to listen to the body's wisdom. The domination of the medical model and the effort to create an autonomous profession out from under the wing of the medical establishment make us reluctant to embrace a biological perspective with unmixed enthusiasm. Furthermore, many social workers are very concerned about and do not want to be identified with the current reductionist view that everything is biological. Our attachment to the rational and the empirical may make us uneasy with the notion of using the wisdom of our own bodies as an avenue to knowing. Again, is our caution cutting us off from a rich source of understanding and helping?

In a third article, William Borden [pp. 135–141] urges us to abandon our single-minded concern with historical truth in assessment and to participate with clients in the construction of narrative truth. Narratives or stories are the "natural cognitive and linguistic forms through which individuals attempt to order, organize, and express meaning." It is the constructed meaning of life events, not the intrinsic nature of the event, that affects our clients, our practice, and ourselves. As Borden points out, "In telling and hearing stories, a person can come to organize and understand experience in ways that help to restore and maintain a sense of coherence and continuity." This constructivist position also stimulates our resistance to giving up both our notion of "the truth" and our reliance on the essential nature of events and history. We have a long history of down-to-earth practical scientism!

These three articles, although affirming different perspectives, have a great deal in common. First, they are radically client-centered as they ask us to listen and to attend in new ways to the deepest, most personal, and most idiosyncratic human experiences. The client is clearly the expert here, thus shifting the hierarchical relationship so common in the therapeutic encounter. It is the client's faith, meanings, and values; the messages from his or her body; and the constructed narrative that directs the work. Second, all three perspectives are health focused in that each explores and makes use of resources within the client that can be available for growth and healing. Finally, each asks us to expand our professional narrative and to entertain other truths. Each fundamentally challenges our basic assumptions—our epistemology.

How will these visions fare in the ongoing development of our professional discourse? Our profession has its story, its preferred narrative that provides us with a shared language and a sense of order, coherence, and continuity. We have our explanatory theories, constructed out of our experience and shaped and constrained by social and political forces. We have long embraced a psychosocial narrative as a way of thinking and of interpreting our experience. In some contexts and periods, the psyche has had more power. Other times we have tended to endow our experience with social meanings. We are not objective or neutral observers; we come with our constructions and shape our experience to be a coherent part of our professional "life story." As Saleebey said, "people tend to follow the path of their expectations."

These expectations and our professional discourse are shaped and constrained by those in power, both in the larger society and in our profession. For example, in the very early years, when the church was a major power, religious views dominated our understanding of clients and their needs. Other powers shape our discourse today: academia, accrediting bodies, funding sources, insurance companies, the changing categories of the *Diagnostic and Statistical Manual of Mental Disorders*, and the national political and social agenda.

We must be alert. We must constantly strive to recognize what these controlling and constraining forces are, and, at times, we must struggle against them. The complex and unknowable human being is our central concern, and we must be open to the many truths that may enhance our understanding, enrich our practice, and empower our clients.

In Search of a Dialogue

The February 1992 annual meeting of the *Social Work* Editorial Board ended with the decision to communicate our vision, our goals, and our plans directly to the readers. Our aim has been to develop a journal that responds to the needs and interests of the membership of the National Association of Social Workers. We have published an increasing number of articles on practice; after all, 63 percent of you are in direct practice. We have also tried to attend to the wide variety of problems faced and settings staffed by professional social workers. We have published articles that focus on the most pressing issues facing our society and our profession.

We also have wanted to provide an opportunity for you to speak to your profession in different ways. We developed two new departments to facilitate this process. In 1990 we inaugurated the Op-Ed column, and since then our journal has been enriched by powerful and personal essays on our nation's and our profession's concerns. A year later we started Notes from the Field, which invites brief descriptions of programs, practice, and research, as the title indicates, rooted in the field. Notes from the

Field was developed primarily so that practitioners could share their work more informally with others of similar interests. These two departments were added to the already existing Points & Viewpoints column, which provides an opportunity for our readers to comment substantively on articles published in the journal. We often ask authors to respond to their critiques.

Finally, we welcome letters to the editor on any topic discussed in the journal or on any issue of concern to the profession. Letters continue the dialogue in a very important way and although not every letter can be published, each is read and considered with great interest.

These are all ways of stimulating and sharing dialogue and of keeping the conversation going on issues important to us all. We hope you find *Social Work* increasingly user-friendly. It does belong to you. We also hope you will join in the dialogue. Let us know what you think. Express your passionate opinions in an Op-Ed. Tell the profession what you are doing in your practice or participate in a dialogue with an author. Join the conversation! *Social Work* is your journal.

Reference

Bateson, G. (1972). *Steps to an ecology of mind.* New York: Ballantine Books.

First published March 1992

In Search of Subjugated Knowledge

I can't say who I am unless you agree I'm real.
—Imamu Amiri Baraka

The above lines simply and eloquently express a vision of knowledge, oppression, power, and truth that have enormous implications for social work practitioners, educators, and researchers. Sharing this poet's vision, postmodern French philosopher Michel Foucault (1980) has taught us that knowledge and power are one, that "we are subjugated to the production of truth through power and we cannot exercise power except through the production of truth" (p. 93).

Social workers, who are deeply concerned about oppressed people, poor people, people of color, women, and people suffering from disabling emotional problems and who are committed to the empowerment of their clients, must examine this intimate power–knowledge relationship. Social workers must reflect on the extent to which we may unwittingly and well-meaningly disempower our clients through our role as "expert," through the authority of our knowledge.

Foucault (1980) studied the development and institutionalization of what he termed "global unitary knowledges" that, through a struggle over time, have come to subjugate a whole set of knowledges and disqualify them as "beneath the required level of cognition or scientificity" (p. 82). In his analysis, the privileging of the methods of science and unitary knowledges have led to the subjugation of previously established erudite knowledge and of local, popular, indigenous knowledge located at the margins of society. These subjugated knowledges have been exiled from the "legitimate domains of formal knowledge" (White & Epston, 1990, p. 26).

Foucault's concern was not only with the centralized political, economic, and institutional regimes that produce privileged knowledges, but also with their exercise of power in the capillaries as they flow out and are practiced at the local level. Or, as Parker (1989) wrote, "The knowledge that circulates in discourse is employed in everyday interaction in relations of submission and domination" (p. 63).

For example, that powerful global and unitary body of knowledge, the *Diagnostic and Statistical Manual of Mental Disorders*, Third Edition (American Psychiatric Association, 1980), which is centrally established and encoded in economic, medical, and educational systems, is practiced at the most local level—in the relationship between a social worker and a client. When a social worker is required by an agency's funding needs or by the rules of third-party payers to attach a diagnostic label to a client, a powerful and privileged classification system has entered this relationship and in all likelihood has affected the worker's thinking, the relationship, and the client's self-definition.

Foucault's (1980) analysis can, perhaps, best be understood through illustrations. The well-known story of how incest has been understood is a dramatic example. After initially thinking that the cause of emotional disturbance in adult women was their being sexually abused as children, Freud came to believe that such memories reported by women were not of real events but were childhood fantasies, evidence of infantile sexual wishes. This scientific knowledge was so reassuring and served such powerful interests that it was maintained for almost 100 years. It was maintained so successfully that the knowledge of incest victims was subjugated to the extent that victims themselves denied their own experience.

Another example of the hegemony of global, unitary knowledge has been the invisibility of women and of people of color in the social sciences, constructed by white males with a few generally marginalized and quieted alternate voices. Other examples include the definition of homosexuality as a disease with resulting elaborate and even destructive protocols for cure and the widely adopted notion of the schizophrenogenic mother and schizophrenic family.

The political nature of knowledge is well illustrated by the fact that each of these privileged truths has been challenged, not primarily by alternative theories from the sciences but by sociopolitical movements that lead to what Foucault (1980) called the insurrection of subjugated knowledge. The women's movement encouraged women to break silence and tell their stories and stimulated the critique of the theory that incest memories were fantasy. The civil rights movement and the rich flowering of African American literature have begun to make visible the African American experience (Collins, 1990). Modern African American women writers are not only bringing forth current subjugated knowledge but are going back to reclaim the ancient knowledges of long-lost early writers such as Zora Neale Hurston and Maria Stewart. In going back these writers are able to connect the historic and current struggles. Gay and lesbian pride, which was sparked by the Stonewall resistance, potentiated the insurrection of yet another subjugated knowledge and the official depathologizing of homosexuality, if not the eradication of homophobia. The mental patients' rights movements and activism on the part of the families of mentally ill people have led to a revision of the discourse about and treatment of mentally ill people and their families.

In each of these examples, oppressed and marginalized populations whose experiences had been described, defined, and categorized by powerful experts rose up to tell their own stories, to bear witness to their own experience, and to define themselves. Through this process, through this insurrection, they have become empowered; and as they have become empowered, their own truths and their own knowledges have begun to be validated and legitimized.

What does this mean for social work practice and research? How can we avoid participating in oppression? How can we lend our efforts to the insurrection of subjugated knowledge and the empowerment of our marginalized client populations?

First, in research and practice we must abandon the role of expert, we must abandon the notion that we are objective observers and our clients are passive subjects to be described and defined. In Foucault's (1980) words,

> We must entertain the claims to attention of local, dis-continuous, disqualified, illegitimate knowledges against the claims of a unitary body of theory which would filter, hierarchize, and order them in the name of some true knowledge and some arbitrary idea of what constitutes a science and its objects. (p. 83)

We must not appropriate those whom we would try to know and understand by "colonizing" their experiences, by interpreting them from the perspective of the privileged expert (Opie, 1992). We must enter into a collaborative search for meaning with our clients and listen to their voices, their narratives, and their constructions of reality. It is significant that studies grounded in the subject's experience, that speak in the voices of oppressed people, and that promote the insurrection of subjugated knowledge have become classics. They are so immediate, so alive, and they teach us so much. Meyerhoff's *Number Our Days* (1978), Liebow's *Tally's Corner* (1968), Erikson's *Everything in Its Path* (1978), and Stack's *All Our Kin* (1974) are such works.

Recently in our own social work literature, Williams (1991) published a volume on black teenage mothers that brings to us their own perspectives, their own experiences, and their own words and presents a very different kind of picture than the large-scale epidemiological studies.

It is really not so complicated; we must ask people and then listen. And as we listen, we must attend to difference, to particularity, the contradictory, the paradoxical. As we do this, we will attend to that which may be quantifiably insignificant but whose presence may question a more conventional interpretation and expand understanding (Opie, 1992). Epidemiological studies are useful and important, but direct practice must be built on local knowledge, on the particular, on attention to difference and, most vital, on multiple voices. The questions to be asked and the interpretations of the data must be developed in collaboration between the researcher or practitioner and the one to be understood who is, after all, the expert. Knowledge and power are one, and when clients and subjects are collaborators in the discovery process, if their expertise is valued and affirmed, they are empowered.

This issue of *Social Work* [November 1992] seems at first to contain a range of somewhat unrelated articles about women, racism, academia, research, and people of color. But if we listen to Foucault, if we agree with him that knowledge is power and power is knowledge, we recognize the deep connection between the empowerment of oppressed people and the development and distribution of knowledge.

There is a painful paradox in being a professional and being committed to empowerment. A key part of the definition of a profession is the possession of knowledge and, in fact, the ownership of a specific area of knowledge. As professionals we are supposed to be experts, but the power in our expertise can disempower our clients and thus subvert the goals of our profession.

How can we resolve this paradox? Must we discard our knowledge, our accumulated professional wisdom? This would leave us adrift without anchor or compass. We need not discard our knowledge, but we must be open to local knowledge, to the narratives and truths of our clients. We must participate with them in the insurrection of subjugated knowledge. We must listen to honor and validate our clients' expertise. We must learn to bracket our knowledge, to put it aside so it will not shape our questions and our listening and cause a barrier between us and the people we would understand. Furthermore, we must not privilege our professional knowledge, and we must let ourselves hear information from our clients that would challenge our views. We must attend. We have been mistaken before and we will be mistaken again. But we are only wrong when we continue to cling to our mistaken truths.

References

American Psychiatric Association. (1980). *Diagnostic and statistical manual of mental disorders* (3rd ed.). Washington, DC: Author.

Baraka, I. A. (1971). Numbers, letters. In D. Randall (Ed.), *The black poets* (p. 218). New York: Bantam Books.

Collins, P. H. (1990). *Black feminist thought: Knowledge, consciousness, and the politics of empowerment.* New York: Unwin Hyman.

Erikson, K. (1978). *Everything in its path: Destruction of community in the Buffalo Creek Flood.* New York: Simon & Schuster.

Foucault, M. (1980). *Power/knowledge: Selected interviews and other writings.* New York: Pantheon Press.

Liebow, E. (1968). *Tally's corner.* Boston: Little Brown.

Meyerhoff, B. (1978). *Number our days.* New York: E. P. Dutton.

Opie, A. (1992, Spring). Qualitative research appropriation of the "other" and empowerment. *Feminist Review, 40,* 52–69.

Parker, I. (1989). Discourse and power. In J. Shotter & K. J. Gergen (Eds.), *Texts of identity* (pp. 56–69). London: Sage Publications.

Stack, C. B. (1974). *All our kin: Strategies for survival in a black community.* New York: Harper & Row.

White, M. & Epston, D. (1990). *Narrative means to therapeutic ends.* New York: W. W. Norton.

Williams, C. W. (1991). *Black teenage mothers: Pregnancy and child rearing from their perspectives.* Lexington, MA: Lexington Books.

First published November 1992

Equity and Justice

Aging Is a Feminist Issue

✣

One of the most remarkable and dramatic changes in our society has been the lengthening of human life. Most people in this country, for the first time in history, will live to be old. Life expectancy at birth has risen from less than 50 years in 1900 to 70 for men and 78 for women in 1985. Women surviving until age 65 can expect to live to 83 and men, to 79. Longevity has increased faster for women than for men; it is predicted that by 1995 there will be 150 women for every 100 men over 65 and 254 women for every 100 men over 84 (Riley, 1985).

What are the implications of these trends? Obviously, the population of older people is growing, and a large proportion of this group will be women. What of the quality of life for this expanding population of older women? Some of these issues are explored in the pages of this journal [September 1990]. First, many older women will be poor or near poor. The term "feminization of poverty" was coined in the late 1970s to describe those social and economic structures and processes that increasingly locked women in poverty. Attention focused primarily on the plight of young mothers and their children (Minkler & Stone, 1985). The feminization of poverty, however, continues throughout the life cycle as demonstrated by Regina O'Grady LeShane in this issue. Institutional sexism and "singleism," structured into our society, assure a woman financial security primarily through her husband's benefits. Many women, it has been said, are but one man away from poverty.

As women get older, widowhood and a life in or near poverty become more likely. Ninety percent of elderly poor women are widowed, divorced, or never married. The roots of the feminization of poverty in old age in our social and economic structure are many. Much of "women's work" has been unpaid and thus without retirement benefits. Working women have been paid less for the same work, have been locked into low-paying jobs in a dual labor market that limits opportunity, and have interrupted work histories with childbearing and rearing responsibilities. As Nelson (1984) pointed out, in our society, "an individual's productive capacity in the market becomes the only legitimate method by which a citizenship-based claim for social benefits can be made" (p. 230). Therefore, women who have had less opportunity to participate in the marketplace and to earn wages receive fewer benefits. Furthermore, although being old and female places one at risk, the poorest segment of American society is elderly black women; 82 percent were poor or near poor at the time of the 1980 census. During Ronald Reagan's trickle-down economic policies of the past decade, the incomes of people at the lowest economic level decreased.

It is likely the 1990 census will show that the economic situation of older white women and women of color has deteriorated further. At the same time, the decimation of social programs, the virtual disappearance of federal support for housing, and the shift of a greater proportion of the cost of health care under Medicare to the recipient in this "kinder and gentler" society have made life even harder for some people, particularly women and people of color (Axin, 1989).

Although modern medical science has extended people's lives, it has not necessarily kept them well. As the numbers of very old people increase, so does the need for personal care and protection. Estimates vary as to the size of this population. A 1982 survey reported in the article by Anastas, Gibeau, and Larson estimated that 2.2 million caregivers were providing unpaid assistance to 1.2 million disabled elderly people. Other estimates go as high as 5 million elderly people in need of some care, and the number is growing (Sammon & Shields, 1987). Most care providers are women. Caregiving to children, the ill, and the elderly has always been women's work, and our society counts on women to carry this burden of unpaid investment in caring. In fact, public policy in the Reagan–Bush years has been "shaped by a hidden agenda based on the ideology of private rather than public provision of services and a commitment to traditional gender roles" (Hess, 1985, p. 319).

Cutbacks in supportive services to maintain elderly people in their homes and in institutional care push more and more family members to assume caretaking responsibilities. As Hess (1985) pointed out with considerable irony,

> The emerging consensus is that frail elderly people should, of course, be cared for at home. Not their home—for that would entail further expenditures in community-based services. . . . Where else but in the home of an adult child? And not just any adult child but the one who can most easily put aside other interests and who is, anyway, equipped by nature to assume this task: the adult daughter. (p. 326)

Humanistic policy supports deinstitutionalization and keeping elderly people in the community. The push has been for family care, but "family" is a euphemism for women, and community care for the elderly depends primarily on the ability and willingness of female family members to provide that care (Walker, 1983).

Women, however, have been moving into the work force, out of necessity or a desire to work, amid widespread concern about caretaking functions. Who will take care of children, aging parents, and chronically disabled family members as women join the labor force? Many working women and some working men continue to provide care for their aging relatives; women in particular suffer considerable stress and conflict as they attempt to manage the demands of employment and caretaking.

Some working women shift some of their caretaking responsibilities to paid home care aides; elderly people without family care available depend on the burgeoning home care industry. This industry survives and in fact may become quite profitable through the exploitation of yet another group of women caregivers. Home care workers are usually poor women of color. "Their employment is best described as marginal; it is characterized by low wages, no health or fringe benefits . . . and there is virtually no opportunity for promotion or advancement" (Donovan, 1987, p. 33). Giving care is not valued in our society.

Caretaking in the family is women's work, and it would appear that caretaking for a wage is black women's work. Gilligan (1982) wrote that women define themselves through relationships and define morality through the ethic of care. Is caring gender-specific, and are women forever destined to carry the burden of caring in our society? As one man in a study on caring commented "Men just don't have the knack for caring for the sick and dying. The 'knack' may, of course, be a lifetime of social expectations" (Sammon & Shields 1987, p. 16).

On many levels, aging is a feminist issue. In the economic and social well-being of aging women, we see the interaction of ageism, sexism, and racism. The only person with less support and protection than an aging white woman alone is an aging woman of color. Employment discrimination, unpaid women's work, and sexist bias in income redistribution leave older women vulnerable; the retrenchment of federal social programs and the shift of resources up the economic scale have made their lives even worse. Furthermore, as public supports shrink and the cost of residential care escalates, more and more frail elderly people, primarily women, require the care of other women—unpaid family members or exploited women of color.

How can the injustice, the inequity, and the deprivation suffered by older women and their caretakers be alleviated? Where are the resources for change?

In one respect, the winds of change may be beginning to increase the extent to which the care ethic is shared by men. Tronto (1987), in her article "Beyond Gender Differences to a Theory of Care," suggested that

> in order for the ethic of care to develop, individuals need to experience caring for others and being cared for by others. From this perspective, the daily experience of caring provides . . . the opportunity to develop this moral sense. The dearth of caretaking experiences makes privileged men morally deprived. (p. 652)

As rigid gender roles shift and men begin to take a more active role in child care, will they begin to value and to share caregiving? This possibility was expressed concretely by a subject in a study of male caregivers:

> Most women have raised children and have more practice in caring for someone. Today, however, if both husband and wife work, both spend equal time raising the kids. These men will then have had more experience when they have to care for the elderly. (Kaye & Applegate, 1990, p. 94)

Researchers have shown that some men are giving care (Kaye & Applegate, 1990). Certainly, the sharing of caregiving responsibilities is an enormously important change; perhaps we will see the day when caregiving is valued human work, not demeaned women's work.

But that is not enough. The personal and the public are intimately connected, and individual men and women cannot sustain care alone in an uncaring society. As long as our nation ignores the needs of a large proportion of our population and as long as the benefits of our society are distributed on the basis of race, sex, age, and class, many of our citizens will not fare well. Perhaps our official attitude toward caregiving was most eloquently demonstrated when President George Bush vetoed the Family Medical Leave Act and Congress sustained his veto. We can hope that this "care-less" message was heard by the caring women and men across this country and that their voices, in turn, will be heard on election day.

References

Axin, J. (1989). Women and aging: Issues of adequacy and equity. *Journal of Women and Aging, 1*(3), 339–362.

Donovan, R. (1987). Home care work: A legacy of slavery in U.S. health care. *Affilia: Journal of Women and Social Work, 2*(3), 33–44.

Gilligan, C. (1982). *In a different voice*. Cambridge, MA: Harvard University Press.

Hess, B. (985). Aging policies and old women: The hidden agenda. In A. S. Rossi (Ed.), *Gender and the life course* (pp. 319–332). New York: Aldine.

Kaye, L., & Applegate, J. (1990). Men as elder caregivers: A response to changing families. *America Journal of Orthopsychiatry, 50*(1), 86–95.

Minkler, M., & Stone, R. (1985). The feminization of poverty and older women. *Gerontologist, 25*(4), 351–357.

Nelson, B. (1984). Women's poverty and women's citizenship: Some political consequences of economic marginality. *Signs, 10*(2), 209–231.

Riley, M. W. (1985). Women, men and the lengthening life course. In A. S. Rossi (Ed.) *Gender and the life course* (pp. 333–348). New York: Aldine.

Sammon, T., & Shields, L. (1987). *Women take care: The consequences of caregiving in today's society.* Gainesville, FL: Triad.

Tronto, J. C. (1987). Beyond gender difference to a theory of care. *Signs, 12*(4), 644–663.

Walker, A. (1983). Care for elderly people: A conflict between women and the state. In J. Finch & D. Graves (Eds.), *A labour of love: Women, work and caring* (pp. 106–128). London: Routledge & Kegan Paul.

First published September 1990

Words Create Worlds

Across the country, college campuses have been resounding with controversy around an issue that has come to be called "political correctness." The term "political correctness" initially was used by hard-line Communists to indicate adherence to the party line and has been adopted as a derisive term for a range of "liberal" attitudes concerning expanded rights and protections for minorities, women, and other oppressed populations. Political correctness is, of course, a crucial issue for social work education. However, although the debate has been centered in academic settings, it has much wider significance.

The current controversy was ignited by the expulsion of a Brown University student for shouting a barrage of racist remarks outside a dormitory late one night. This event focused attention on the efforts of universities to censure or punish students and faculty for harassing statements or behaviors directed at particular racial, ethnic, or gender groups.

Some students began to protest that such actions on the part of colleges and universities violated the First Amendment—the right of free speech—and challenged academic freedom. As the debate intensified, conservative Republican Representative Henry Hyde introduced a bill into Congress—the collegiate Speech Protection Act of 1991—as an amendment to the Civil Rights Act of 1964. This act challenges the growing number of college behavior codes that have been developing in response to the upsurge of racial and sexual tensions and harassment on college campuses. These behavior codes are developed by university administrators to create a climate of civility on campuses.

In a decision, on September 7, 1989, the U.S. District Court struck down a University of Michigan harassment code. The judge ruled that it "swept within its scope a significant amount of 'verbal conduct' or 'verbal behavior' which is unquestionably protected by the First Amendment" (Talbot, 1991). The Hyde bill would extend this principle to private colleges and universities, excluding those under the auspices of religious organizations.

The lines have been sharply drawn: the right to freedom of speech versus the right not to be denigrated, threatened, or harassed. This matter involves more than just conservative and liberal positions, and the complexity of the issue has led to some strange bedfellows. For example, the liberal American Civil Liberties Union (ACLU) has joined conservatives in support of this bill. In justifying this position, ACLU President Nadine Strossen stated that the ACLU "is extremely troubled by the upsurge of racial incidents and bias" but that speech codes "are an unprincipled as well as an unconstitutional way of dealing with racism" ("Bill Aims," 1991).

Perhaps the discussion of political correctness has opened up an arena for new levels of argument and discussion that, it is hoped, will lead to a more complex and subtle interpretation of the meanings of the rights and freedoms involved. Currently, the argument surrounding this issue repeatedly escalates to a struggle between two absolutes: freedom of speech and protection from harm. Clearly, both of these rights are relative; that is, they shift in meaning with changing times and contexts. Discussions more usefully revolve around the extent to which freedom of speech must be limited when it interferes with the rights and welfare of others and the extent to which discomfort, unpleasantness, and even offensive ideas and language must be tolerated so that freedom of speech can be protected appropriately. A judgment can be made only if these two relative rights are carefully balanced.

In attempting to explore this balance, it is essential to recognize the power of language. People who elevate freedom of speech tend to trivialize this power. Such trivialization was dramatic in Hyde's description of his bill, which was intended, in his words, "to prevent you from getting kicked out of school if you said something unpopular or that offends somebody" ("Bill Aims," 1991).

Discounting the power of language contradicts major developments in current social science theory that have been grouped under the term "post-modernism" or "constructivism." Postmodernists believe that words not only reflect but also shape our world and that we cannot know our world except through the languages we have created to define, describe, and interpret it. Our shared ideas about reality are social constructions or products of social discourses that emerge out of and also shape social processes.

Furthermore, as French philosopher Michel Foucault (1980) suggested, not all interpretations, not all stories, and not all social discourses are equal. There is a recursive relationship between knowledge, or rather social discourse that has come to be termed knowledge, and power. The words, interpretations, languages, and social discourses of people in power tend to become privileged and accepted as truth or knowledge, whereas the discourses of disempowered people tend to become marginalized. The voices of disempowered people become subjugated and silenced and their stories are untold.

A postmodern analysis of the free speech versus human welfare debate casts the issue in a very different light. People in power can maintain that power through their control of knowledge and through their ability to define reality and to marginalize or subjugate other views of the world. Clearly "names" or "naming" can inflict irreparable harm. Throughout recorded history, individuals and entire groups of people have been "languaged" as inferior, subversive, or evil. Such discourses, as they gain hegemony, have been used to justify a range of social punishments from isolation to genocide.

The dominant social discourses in our society have tended to be racist, sexist, and homophobic. The voices of people of color, women, lesbians and gay men, and other diverse groups, until very recently, have gone unheard. In the current struggle over political correctness, two opposing discourses have emerged. One is an effort by people whose views have been marginalized to delegitimize racism, sexism, and other oppressive discourses and to define such language as unacceptable. The other is a growing effort to disempower this strategy by terming it "an extraordinarily potent effort in academia to stifle dissenters from what has come to be known on campuses around the U.S. as Politically Correct views" ("Politically Correct," 1990, p. A10).

In the postmodernist view, speech is an action, not simply a reflection. Words carry intentionality. Thus, in postmodern terms we must ask "What ends does this discourse serve?" or, more simply, "What are they trying to do by saying what they are saying?"

We must put this question to those people who have launched or joined the campaign against political correctness. Are they simply defending freedom of speech, or are they using the power of words to once again subjugate the voices of oppressed people, to leave them unprotected, and to encourage the current atmosphere of backlash?

As we struggle with this issue, the concerns about academic freedom and about limitations on freedom of speech cannot be put aside. The United States has just been through a war during which information was controlled aggressively and freedom of the press was curtailed. In a recent commencement address, President George Bush, speaking on the issue of political correctness, stated that freedom of speech "may be the most fundamental and deeply revered of all our liberties" (Dowd, 1991). Such reverence may be tempered, depending on which subject is to be discussed freely. Freedom of speech is vital on all topics of concern to Americans. Information is power, and without adequate information we are helpless. Certainly, the First Amendment must be guarded and freedom of inquiry and diversity of opinion protected in our institutions of learning.

We must not be forced into a dichotomous position. We must preserve a stance that includes both the conviction that all people must be protected from demeaning harassment and from being disparaged and marginalized and the conviction that freedom of speech must be protected. In taking such a stance, it is necessary to consider each situation on its own merits and to find a balance between the two rights.

This issue has important implications for social work education and practice. Social work programs are located in institutions that are debating the issues and thus are involved in the conflict. In a value-laden profession that is committed to social justice and the empowerment of oppressed people, does a social work educator have a perspective on the issue of academic freedom that is different from other academicians? Where do we stand when academic freedom is used to subvert the values of the profession?

Some colleges and universities have come under attack for requiring courses in social justice, racism, or women's issues. Such content is required in the Council on Social Work Education's accreditation standards for all social work programs. The goals of professional education are not identical to those of the liberal arts or the sciences; thus, social work educators, certainly not for the first time, may find themselves at odds with some of their colleagues.

Social work practitioners must never discount the power of language. Indeed, we, along with people who are oppressed, must continue to challenge the dominant discourses that attempt to marginalize groups on the basis of such categories as color, sex, age, or sexual orientation. We must participate in the efforts of such groups to claim the right to define themselves and their experiences—that is, to describe their own lives (Collins, 1989; Laird, 1989).

The controversy surrounding political correctness is not over. Social workers can bring to the debate an appreciation of our heritage of freedom and our first-hand knowledge of and concern for the oppressed and marginalized people who suffer when such freedoms are abused.

References

Bill aims at relaxing rules for racial slurs on campus. (1991, March 13). *New York Times*.

Collins, P. (1989). The social construction of black feminist thought. *Signs: A Journal of Women in Contemporary Society, 14,* 745–773.

Dowd, M. (1991, May 5). President warns against stifling of campus ideas. *New York Times*.

Foucault, M. (1980). *Power/knowledge*. New York: Pantheon Books.

Laird, J. (1989). Women and stories: Restorying women's self-constructions. In M. McGoldrick, C. Anderson, & F. Walsh (Eds.), *Women in families: A framework for family therapy* (pp. 427–450). New York: W. W. Norton.

Politically correct. (1990, November 26). *Wall Street Journal*,
  p. A1.
Talbot, B. (1991, March 11). Odd allies fight conduct codes.
  Chicago Sun Times.

First published July 1991

It Was Not Our Finest Hour

The weeks have grown into months since the tragedy and drama of the Clarence Thomas confirmation hearings. Thomas has taken his seat on the highest court in the land, and Anita Hill has returned to the University of Oklahoma. The hearings are over, but those who were touched by them as participants and as observers will never be the same.

Thomas joins the court with narrow support, compromised by the suspicions the hearings failed to calm and by his handling of the accusations. Hill, although fortunately supported by her university and community, will in all likelihood not be sought out for appointments to other leadership positions. She, too, will forever carry, in the minds of some, the mark of suspicion. As for the other participants, the Senate and the Supreme Court have never commanded so little confidence and respect from the American people. Both parties are under fire, the Republican for its treatment of Hill, the Democratic for its fumbling and incompetent handling of the entire affair.

Those who watched the drama unfold, who were both mesmerized and horrified by the proceedings, will never be the same. Who can blot out the image of Hill—calm, courageous, dignified—facing 14 white men? Who can forget the tragedy of the two proud and successful black Americans facing each other in an arena surrounded by white people? Who cannot return to these events to reflect, to consider and reconsider, to try to understand, to come to terms, to try to fashion some plan of action? We will never be the same, because the drama brought to the surface the deepest conflicts and most painful struggles in

American society. The hearings were about gender and race and, in the end, about power and oppression. The underside of our social order was exposed. It was not our finest hour.

There were bitter lessons. We learned that sexual harassment does not matter—that it is not important, that it is not to be taken seriously. We learned that the lawmakers of this land have no understanding of sexual harassment, of what it is or of how it is defined, and that many did not even know the law. When reports of allegations reached the Judiciary Committee, they were ignored or even hushed up. It was only the leak to the press, the fact that the charges were made public, and finally the overwhelming tide of outrage rising up from women all over the country that forced the committee to postpone the confirmation vote and to investigate Hill's charges.

We also learned how men will join together to defend each other when one of their own is called to account. Why could the Democrats not defend Hill? Why did they bring her forth and then abandon her? These trained lawyers acted, as one national magazine stated, like a bunch of opossums caught in a car's headlights. Their cross-examination was totally ineffective. They failed to question Thomas on his well-documented interest in pornographic films and never countered spurious psychiatric allegations directed at Hill by bringing forth experts that could destroy such testimony. Why were they so inept? Did they agree on some level that it was no big deal, that a man's career should not be destroyed by such a minor thing that happened so long ago? Or were some thinking, "There but for the grace of God go I"? The only truly eloquent spokesman in support of Hill was Ted Kennedy, but his impassioned cry of shame had a hollow ring in the context of his own personal life.

And we learned about power and about the uses and abuses of power. Most thinking people, the senators excluded, came to understand that sexual harassment is not about sex or about asking someone for a date, it is about power, and that "sexual harassment is a form of social control which has the aim of maintaining the dominance of men" (Maypole, 1987, p. 26). Hill was repeatedly asked, "Why didn't you come forward? Why didn't you leave your job?" Such naive questions illustrate the inability of 14 of the most privileged and powerful white men in the land to understand what it is like to be powerless, to be in the beginning of a career that had been bought at the price of enormous hard work and personal and family sacrifice, and to be afraid to jeopardize that career. Why did Frances Conley, a neurosurgeon on the Stanford University Medical School faculty, wait 25 years to speak out? The power differential in situations of sexual harassment dictates that the accuser has more to lose than the accused.

But we did not only learn about the abuse of power in harassment; we learned about the abuse of power by members of the Senate. The use of dirty tricks and the deliberate attack on the character, motives, mental condition, and veracity of Hill were horrifying. We witnessed the abuse of power by President George Bush, who could have kept hands off and allowed the process to work even if it meant choosing another candidate. Instead, Bush chose "to push Clarence Thomas onto the Court by any available means, to win at any cost, to place political victory ahead of presidential responsibility" (Wicker, 1991).

We have also once again been reminded of the powerlessness of women in our society. The lack of concern about sexual harassment is frightening in the context of escalating violence against women in the home and on the street, the epidemic of rape, and the blatant sexism beamed into our homes every day on commercial television. There can be no social justice and no "representative" government as long as power and resources are almost exclusively in the hands of white men. The Senate is composed of 98 men and 2 women; the House, 406 men and 29 women. The gains made in the 1960s and 1970s through the women's movement have been eroding under two administrations that have consistently worked to turn back the clock. Programs and policies of concern to women and essential to women's welfare have been consistently opposed, including family leave, day care, reproductive rights, and affirmative action. Faludi's (1991) chilling account *Backlash: The Undeclared War against American Women* not only reported the erosion of the small gains by women made in previous decades but also documented the frightening manipulation of public opinion and of the truth through defining the goals of the women's movement as destructive to women themselves. This subtle and pernicious backlash has "managed to infiltrate the thoughts of women, broadcasting on these private channels its soundwaves of shame and reproach" (p. 455).

And it is with shame and reproach, and I might add guilt, that women are silenced, that their voice, and thus their truth and their power, are taken from them. Why did Hill not come forward? Why do we not all come forward and speak out? Partly it is fear, but partly it is shame and the deep feeling of responsibility women feel for relationship.

Hill finally and reluctantly came forward, but in doing so, she broke deeply held taboos. In a brilliant essay, Bray (1991) described the wrenching conflict between loyalty to her race and gender Hill must have experienced as she finally spoke. She "put her private business in the street, and she downgraded a black man to a room filled with white men who might alter his fate— surely a large enough betrayal for her to be read out of the race" (p. 94).

Thomas evoked one of the most powerful and emotional images in African American consciousness when he accused his accusers of "high-tech lynching." Hill could have evoked another painful image—that of the centuries of sexual abuse of black women, slave and free—but she did not. As Bray commented, it would have been more enlightening for the senators (and indeed for us all) to have read *Incidents in the Life of a Slave Girl* than the *Exorcist* in providing a context for the hearings.

Hill, as a black woman, had a special reason to be silent, but all women have been silenced and disempowered through that silencing. Another shameful moment in the hearings was the repudiation of her testimony through "expert" evidence from a psychiatrist that this could all be a product of fantasy. We are familiar with this strategy. For 100 years, incest survivors were told that their memories were fantasy and evidence of their own sexual wishes. It was agonizing to hear this silencing strategy go unchallenged.

Thus, people in power define the truth and use that power to define those who challenge those truths as foolish, mistaken, manipulated, or crazy. Women have not been in power. They have been silenced through complex social and cultural processes and thus are further disempowered (Laird, in press).

What can we do? To what plan of action can these painful lessons lead us? First, in the world of social work we must establish in every social agency and in every school of social work procedures for exposing and dealing with harassment. But that is not enough. We must make sure that everyone knows of the procedures and the protections available against sexual harassment. In one study, 77 percent of the students in a school of social work did not know that such procedures were in place (Maypole, 1987). In addition, we must establish an atmosphere that makes it possible for all those who suffer harassment to come forth. We must help them gain their voice. In our practice, we must listen with care to our clients and help them tell us about the degradation they have experienced. They will need encouragement to voice their fears and their disgust. And they need more than just a sympathetic ear. They need help planning ways to empower themselves to get into a position in which they will not be forced to suffer such harassment. And we must be vigilant in monitoring our profession. Because we are in positions of power with our clients, we must intervene firmly and forcefully in any situation in which clients suffer harassment by social workers.

But we must look beyond our own work lives and beyond the issue of harassment to the inequities in the distribution of power in our society. We must challenge the Senate as a white men's club. We must seek opportunity at every level of government to support women and people of color for office. We must run for office ourselves. Social work is an excellent training ground for a career in politics, and social workers are holding office nationwide. How proud we can be of Barbara Mikulski, senator from Maryland and a social worker, when she speaks so forcefully. But her voice is clearly a lonely one and must be joined by others. We learned much from the Thomas hearing; perhaps the most important lesson is that there can be no justice in this diverse nation as long as political power remains the almost undisputed property of white men.

References

Bray, R. (1991, November 17). Taking sides against ourselves. *New York Times Magazine*, p. 56.

Faludi, S. (1991). *Backlash: The undeclared war against American women*. New York: Crown.

Laird, J. (in press). Women's secrets, women's silences. In E. I. Black (Ed.), *Secrets in family therapy*. New York: W. W. Norton.

Maypole, D. (1987). Sexual harassment at work: A review of research and theory. *Affilia, 2*, 24–38.

Wicker, T. (1991, October 17). A glorious victory. *New York Times*, p. 27.

First published January 1992

A Message from Los Angeles

All is quiet in Los Angeles, at least on the surface. It is an uneasy silence. The wounds are deep, and the devastation wrought by the explosion of rage and anguish following the Rodney King verdict is very much in evidence. The presidential candidates and Congress, after years of looking the other way, are competing over who has the best plan to address the problems of the inner city, responding to the polls that, at least for the moment, are suggesting Americans want something done.

A message has been sent to the nation from Los Angeles, a message that has raised our national consciousness and to which we must respond. It has been said that if you want to see our future, look to Los Angeles.

What we saw in Los Angeles were tremors caused by three deep faults in the bedrock of American society: poverty, lack of opportunity, and racism. These faults leave our land vulnerable to a cataclysm as surely as does the San Andreas Fault that lies beneath California.

Poverty

First, in this nation so rich in resources, millions continue to live in grinding, depriving, demeaning poverty. The situation has steadily deteriorated in the past decade as the gap between the rich and the poor has grown to be greater than at any time since statistics have been kept. By 1988, the average annual income of the 10 percent of American families at the bottom of the economic ladder was $3,504, while the top 1 percent averaged $404,566, reflecting an increase in real dollars of almost 50 percent in a decade (Phillips, 1990).

We must not delude ourselves that poverty in the inner cities is a result of the current recession, although increased unemployment has exacerbated the situation. We must also not delude ourselves that this change in our economic structure was the result of some inevitable social Darwinian dynamics. The change was the outcome of purposeful economic and social policies of the Reagan–Bush administration. First, it was a result of Ronald Reagan's famous "trickle-down" theory of economics. It was Reagan's view that if more capital were available to those at the top of the economic ladder, entrepreneurship and investment would be encouraged, thereby stimulating the economy; the benefits of an improved economy would trickle down to working people and poor people.

As we know well, Reagan's optimistic predictions did not come to pass. The rich got richer, but the economy did not grow as expected. The poor got poorer, and by the end of 1984, the deficit accumulated by the Reagan administration had surpassed the deficits of all preceding American presidents combined (Jansson, 1988).

George Bush continues to promote similar policies, as exemplified in his campaign to reduce the capital gains tax and in his "read my lips" promise, which brings cheers from the hard-pressed middle and working classes but primarily benefits those in the top 5 percent who continue to pick up such a small share of the national tax burden.

Lack of Opportunity

The second great fault in American society is the inequality of opportunity and the fact that millions of Americans are excluded from the opportunity structure. Rodney King was even excluded from the benefits of the justice system.

The events in Los Angeles reminded us of the riots of the 1960s that spread from city to city and turned our attention to the War on Poverty programs developed in response to the growing civil unrest. President Bush, for example, thinking about the 1960s while touring Los Angeles, blamed the War on Poverty programs for the situation in the inner cities. He invoked the ultraconservative position explicated by Murray (1984), whose *Losing Ground* provided the conceptual underpinning for Reagan's attack on the poor population. Murray contended that social welfare programs cause poverty, rather than reduce it, and also cause joblessness, crime, out-of-wedlock births, female-headed families, and welfare dependency, undermining the norms and aspirations of the urban poor population, sapping their incentive to work and to maintain stable families.

The social theory that fueled the War on Poverty was opportunity theory, or anomie theory. Developed in the 19th century by the French father of sociology, Emile Durkheim (1951), in his classic *Suicide* and elaborated by Robert Merton (1957), anomie theory hypothesizes that "aberrant behavior may be regarded sociologically as a symptom of disassociation between culturally prescribed aspirations and socially structured avenues for realizing these aspirations" (Merton, 1957, p. 132).

When people are locked out of the opportunity structure and thus unable to realize universally held aspirations, they may adapt to this societal double bind in four ways. They may abandon their aspirations and live a conforming life of deprivation and disappointment. They may cling to their aspirations but abandon the social structure, innovating illegitimate opportunities to achieve their aspirations. They may abandon both aspirations and social structures and retreat into alcoholism, drugs, depression, or suicide. Or they may act as revolutionaries to bring about change in society and to open up the opportunity structure.

The programs of the New Frontier and the Great Society sought to open up opportunity and to change the social structure through broad citizen participation, training and education, job development, legal services, affirmative action, and a wide range of community-based programs established to bring those who had been excluded into the mainstream.

Although there can be grave doubt that Bush has been reading his Durkheim, theorists have warned that anomie intensifies when hope is kindled, aspirations heightened, and promises made and then broken. In that sense, the desperation in the inner cities may well be related to the Great Society programs, not because they undermined initiative but rather because they kindled hope and aspiration and then failed. They failed, primarily, not because they were poorly conceived, but because support was withdrawn, because our resources and our attention became mired in the Vietnam War.

But why indiscriminate violence? Why not revolution, as Durkheim would have predicted in situations of such disappointment and disillusionment?

Durkheim, perhaps, could not conceive of the undermining, pacifying, disorganizing effects of widespread substance abuse. The distribution and use of drugs make an enormously effective instrument of social control. By altering consciousness, deadening pain, and covering despair, drugs sap the energy, the capacity, and the motivation to organize and to revolt to demand major social change. There has been a great deal of talk about the War on Drugs, but it has not been followed by effective action. A cynic may ask, "Could it be that those in power are not anxious to win that war, that the distribution of drugs in the inner city anesthetizes the disconnected and deadens the revolutionary spirit, thus contributing to the maintenance of the status quo?"

Racism

The third fault in our society is racism, which has undermined our national moral position and put the lie to our vision of freedom and justice since the first ship landed bringing Africans into slavery. Scholars debate whether it is current racism or the cumulative effects of centuries of prejudice and discrimination that have created an impenetrable barrier between many people of color and opportunity (Wilson, 1987); it is probably the combined influence of both. The civil rights revolution, desegregation, and affirmative action have taken us a step or two closer, but we still have a long road to travel before racism is truly eradicated from our society.

Our Response

How can we respond to the message from Los Angeles? We must begin to mend the great faults that cause so much hopelessness and suffering and that leave our nation so vulnerable. Bush's six-point program, developed in response to the crisis in Los Angeles, once again demonstrates his unwillingness to genuinely tackle the problems of the poor. Some proposals are utterly mystifying; one example is allowing parents to use tax money to pay for private schools. Wouldn't such a plan increase the isolation of the poor population in bankrupt inner-city schools?

Another proposal that will help very few is the plan to allow families on welfare to save up to $10,000 without threatening their eligibility. The notion that people on welfare can save $10,000 demonstrates how far our leaders are from understanding the situation of those in poverty. Job training and public housing proposals are seriously underfunded, as is the program proposal to "weed out criminals" and "seed" the cities with social services.

Of greatest concern is the fact that programs that only tinker with the system probably will not mean any real transfer of resources to poor people, because the cost is to come out of existing programs, heightening the resentment and competition among groups in need.

How should we respond to the message from Los Angeles? First, we must change the direction of our national policy by changing our leadership on the national, state, and local levels. We must take advantage of the opportunity offered by the 1992 elections; actively join the political process; and support candidates who give evidence of pursuing goals of equal opportunity, social justice, and the eradication of poverty and racism. The tax system must be reformed and priorities altered so that the burden is shared progressively in relation to income. Transfers must be made to reduce the gap between the rich and the poor, and the long-awaited peace dividend must be increased and used to reduce our national debt and to finance social programs.

Second, we must open up the opportunity structure to those who are excluded and prepare them to enter that structure. It is fashionable to be critical of the War on Poverty programs, but perhaps we can be old-fashioned enough to reconsider the principles on which the programs were based and to use what we learned in that innovative period to create new avenues of opportunity for all Americans.

Finally, we must renew our commitment to combat racism whenever it appears: in the workplace, in educational institutions, in the political world, and in our own profession. We must support the now-embattled principles of affirmative action and not be fooled by backlash strategies such as the "political correctness" attack. We must not let ourselves succumb to hopelessness, disillusionment, and anomie. One committed person can make a difference, and many committed people joining together in a just cause can turn this country around. Let's make the crisis in Los Angeles not a threat, but an opportunity.

References

Durkheim, E. (1951). *Suicide* (J. A. Spaulding & G. Simpson, Trans.). New York: Free Press.

Jansson, B. S. (1988). *The reluctant welfare state: A history of American social welfare policies*. Belmont, CA: Wadsworth.

Merton, R. K. (1957). *Social theory and social structure*. Glencoe, IL: Free Press.

Murray, C. (1984). *Losing ground: American social policy 1950–1980*. New York: Basic Books.

Phillips, K. (1990). *The politics of the rich and the poor: Wealth and the American electorate in the Reagan aftermath*. New York: Random House.

Wilson, W. J. (1987). *The truly disadvantaged: The inner city, the underclass, and public policy*. Chicago: University of Chicago Press.

First published July 1992

Out of the Closet:
Revolution and Backlash

The growing conflict concerning the status of gay men and lesbians in the armed forces has become a focal point in the long, slow struggle toward equal rights for this stigmatized and oppressed segment of American society. The issue is a metaphor for the position long occupied by gay men and lesbians. Although it is well known that thousands of homosexuals serve in the armed forces, as long as they hide their sexual orientation, as long as they neither name it nor claim it, everyone can pretend they are not there, that they don't exist. It appears that it is not being gay or lesbian that brings wrath down on service personnel, but voicing it.

Colin Powell, the former chairman of the Joint Chiefs of Staff who has led the fight against President Bill Clinton's commitment to eliminate discrimination against gays in the armed forces, claims that the president's position is very different than that of Truman when he ended the policy of racial segregation in the armed forces 45 years ago. In this situation, Powell argues, it is a question of behavior (Schmitt, 1993). The military's right to have an on-duty behavioral code for all service personnel, however, is not being challenged. The issue is not behavior, it is disclosure; it is the threat and the challenge posed when people come out of the closet. There is no better way to subjugate human beings than to silence them. There is nothing more oppressive than denying another's reality.

Until the Stonewall demonstration and the birth of the gay liberation movement, lesbians and gay men survived through secrecy—and most still do. The cost was and continues to be great. As murdered gay sailor Allen Schindler poignantly wrote in his diary, "If you can't be yourself, then who are you?" ("Diary," 1993).

Forced to be invisible, without rights or protections, gay men and lesbians have been personally and politically disempowered. In his book, *Gays/Justice*, Mohr (1988) explored the relationship between invisibility, powerlessness, and social change. He wrote,

> Only when the government protects gays against discrimination in housing, employment, and public accommodation will gays have first amendment rights as powers. For all potentially effective political strategies involve *public* actions. More specifically, all the actions protected by the first amendment are public actions (speaking, publishing, petitioning, assembling, associating). Now, a person who is a member of an invisible minority and who must remain invisible, hidden, and secreted in respect to her minority status . . . is effectively denied all political power. . . . (p. 173)

Thus, for gay men and lesbians to become politically active and to fight for their rights and protection, they must be safe enough to become visible; they are only safe to do so if those rights and protections are already in place—an immobilizing paradox.

The same situation exists in the personal world. The closeted condition of gay men and lesbians blocks understanding. "Social reality is such that many people . . . think they do not know any gay people firsthand. Such widespread ignorance is a breeding ground for vicious stereotypes" (Mohr, 1988, p. 176). Such invisibility and powerlessness made it possible for Chief Justice Warren Burger to say, after the Supreme Court decision upholding the Georgia sodomy laws, that he had never personally known a gay person (Sedgwick, 1988, p. 44). The best way to change heterosexuals' views about gay men and lesbians is for them to interact personally with openly gay people. "Coming out," then, is an enormously powerful personal and political act.

The courageous pioneers who came forward have taken great risks. But that was the message of Stonewall: Stand up, be counted, fight back. Every year, marches commemorating Stonewall give people an opportunity to stand up and be counted. As this article went to press, the planned April 25 march on Washington promised to be the largest demonstration to date of the increasing power of the gay rights movement.

Stonewall was the beginning, but it was the acquired immune deficiency syndrome (AIDS) epidemic that was to bring together gays and lesbians across the country. The AIDS epidemic presents a crisis of such dimensions that gay men and lesbians have taken the risks, found their voices, and organized to demand resources to care for the sick, to fight the disease, and to search for treatment.

In meeting this challenge, gay men and lesbians have discovered their power and have launched a social revolution. The markers of that revolution, large and small, are all around us: the smiling faces of two young women on the front page of the *New York Times* celebrating their commitment and the public validation of their relationship as they register as domestic partners on the first day it became possible in New York City; the visible presence of more than 100 gay and lesbian delegates to the Democratic National Convention; the provision of health insurance to same-sex partners of employees by several municipalities, universities, and private companies; an article in the *Times* reporting that public schools across the country are cautiously adding materials on gay life (Celis, 1993); the publication of research and scholarly works that explore the gay and lesbian world from a nondeficit, nonpathological perspective, finding, for example, that children raised in gay and lesbian families do at least as well as children raised in heterosexual families and that lesbian and gay families have special strengths (Laird, in press; Weston, 1991); the reinstatement of Petty Officer Keith Meinhold; the passage of statutes in six states and 110 municipalities barring discrimination against gays and lesbians (Schmalz, 1992); the reversal of historic precedent in the sentencing of Brown and Becci to 25 years in prison for the gay hate murder of Julio Rivera after $1^1/_2$ years of advocacy by gay activists (Minkowitz, 1992); and the court ruling in New York State that allows gay men and lesbians to legally adopt children (Marks, 1992).

How far will this sea change carry us? Lesbians and gay men are pressing for equity and for a federal civil rights law that would protect them from discrimination in employment, housing, public accommodations, and education, eligibility for credit, and other utilities and services. Gay men and lesbians are also seeking not merely toleration but acceptance and the recognition and support of their families.

But for every action, there is a reaction. Every social revolution that redistributes power, that challenges deeply held beliefs, and that presses for attention to subjugated knowledge will be met with resistance and backlash. This social revolution has been launched in a context that is at best lukewarm, at worst viciously hostile. American opinions on this issue, as polls have shown, are both deeply divided and ambivalent. Although a recent poll found that 80 percent of Americans believe that lesbians and gay men should have equal employment opportunities and 57 percent felt they should be free to serve in the military, only 38 percent thought that homosexuality was an acceptable alternate lifestyle, and only 38 percent believed that homosexual relations between consenting adults should be legal (Schmalz, 1992, p. 41). The message is clear: Homosexuals may work and serve, but they may not love.

Similar inconsistency is reflected in the growing hostility toward gay men and lesbians. Although a step forward creates hope, the resistance, anger, and hatred remind us of the depth, intensity, and pervasiveness of homophobia. Setbacks have been many. Particularly shocking was the 1986 Supreme Court decision in *Bowers v. Hardwick* that the privacy doctrine developed in previous cases to protect families and marital couples as well as individuals did not include homosexual conduct between consenting adults. The court thus upheld Georgia's sodomy laws and, by extension, the sodomy laws still existing in 23 other states. This is in direct opposition to the finding by the European Court, in the case of *Dudgeon v. United Kingdom*, which ruled that the existence of Northern Irish statutes concerning homosexual behavior, even if not enforced, infringed on the plaintiff's private life and were, therefore, in violation of the European Convention. Most of the nations in the Council of Europe had already abolished criminal penalties for homosexual acts between consenting adults (Glendon, 1991).

American inconsistency in this area is dramatically demonstrated by the fact that a mere 18 months before the Supreme Court held that homosexual behavior was not protected as "private," the Court found against a guidance counselor who had been fired after she disclosed her sexual orientation to a few colleagues, because "the act of coming out was judged not to be protected under the first amendment because it did not constitute speech on a matter of public concern" (Sedgwick, 1988, p. 42). It seems that homosexuality can be constructed as neither public nor private and thus is ineligible for any protection.

But beyond the inconsistency and double-binding oppression has been a growing chorus of hostility and escalating violence. Low points include the homophobic attacks at the Republican Convention ("Malice toward Some," 1992) and the passage in Colorado of an amendment to the state constitution designed to eliminate protection for gays, followed by a burst of antigay activities, hate crimes, and firings (Zeman & Meyer, 1992). Violence against gay men and lesbians appears to be on the increase. There are reports of continued police and judicial indifference (Baker, 1991), such as Dallas Judge Jack Hampton's comment upon giving the killer of two gay men a light sentence. "I put prostitutes and queers at the same level" (Rist, 1990, p. 483). Less visible but equally destructive is the continued harassment, isolation, and dismissal of avowed homosexuals in many workplaces, as well as the pervasive day-by-day and private unknown expressions of hate and homophobia encountered by lesbians and gay men everywhere and encountered by those who speak out against intolerance.

The specific and known is perhaps the most painful. Recently, the 13-year-old son of a friend was changing for swimming in the locker room of a junior high school located in a university community. He became rather peripherally involved in a heated argument over service of gays in the military. When one of the boys announced, "All gays should be killed," the son of my friend commented rather quietly, "That was a rather homophobic comment," and went off swimming. When he returned to the locker room, he found that someone had urinated all over his clothes and his book bag. Perhaps most painful was the response of the school officials. Although expressing caring and concern, they felt helpless and saw no way to intervene or to shift the climate of the school.

Where is social work in this social revolution? This is a question we must all ask ourselves. Social work's historical mission has been to work in behalf of oppressed peoples. Some leaders in the profession have pressed for attention to the oppression and the welfare of gay men and lesbians. We have moved with the DSM away from diagnosing homosexuality as an illness. There is an occasional paper on the topic presented at professional conferences or published in professional journals. Some schools of social work and agencies include sexual orientation in their nondiscrimination statements. Finally, after years of discussion, the Council on Social Work Education now requires that content on gay men and lesbians be included in each school's curriculum.

Adherence to our mission and to our values demands that the profession take a stronger and more proactive position on the individual, organizational, and educational levels. First, on the individual level, every social worker must recognize that we have all grown up in a heterosexist society, and we must face within ourselves the residue of living in a homophobic world. Secondly, we must become aware of the rather universal ignorance about gay men and lesbians, put aside our presuppositions, definitions, and theories, and listen to their own stories, their own understandings, which, like narratives of the black experience, have been subjugated. We must advocate on their behalf.

Each individual must also examine her or his own agency or organization for oppressive policies or subtle hostility and work proactively to change such policies. Has anyone on the staff come out? If so, how has it been for them? If not, why not? What would happen if someone did? Does the agency or organization include sexual orientation in their anti-discrimination statement? Why not? Are there gay and lesbian clients? If not, why not? If so, how are they understood and treated? Is sexual orientation considered their problem? In schools of social work, is up-to-date content on gay men and lesbians integrated in courses, or is it tacked on the end of a syllabus, in a unit that the class somehow never gets to, or is it offered as an elective? How do identified gay men and lesbians fare at admission? These are just a few of the many questions we must ask ourselves.

On the national level, we must press NASW to take on the issue of gay rights more actively and to make the weight of our profession felt by those who would reverse the movement toward acceptance and equity for gay men and lesbians.

References

Baker, J. N. (1991, November 25). Battling the bias. *Newsweek*, p. 25.

Celis, W. (1993, January 6). Schools across the U.S. cautiously adding lessons on gay life. *New York Times*, p. A7.

Diary: A sailor's private torment. (1993, February 1). *Newsweek*, p. 57.

Glendon, M. A. (1991). *Rights talk: The impoverishment of political discourse*. New York: Free Press.

Laird, J. (in press). Lesbians in gay families. In F. Walsh (Ed.), *Normal family processes*. New York: Guilford Press.

Malice toward some. (1992, October 26). *New Yorker*, pp. 4–5.

Marks, J. D. (1992, February 1). A victory for the new American family. *New York Times*, p. 21.

Minkowitz, D. (1992, March 30). It's still open season on gays. *Nation*, pp. 368–370.

Mohr, R. D. (1988). *Gays/justice: A study of ethics, society, and law*. New York: Columbia University Press.

Rist, D. (1990, April 9). Homosexuals and human rights. *Nation*, pp. 482–484.

Schmalz, J. (1992, October 11). Gay politics goes mainstream. *New York Times Magazine*, pp. 18–21.

Schmitt, E. (1993, January 23). Joint chiefs fighting Clinton plan to allow homosexuals in the military. *New York Times*, p. 12.

Sedgwick, E. K. (1988, Spring). Epistemology of the closet. *Raritan*, pp. 39–69.

Weston, K. (1991). *Families we choose: Lesbian and gay kinship*. New York: Columbia University Press.

Yang, J. E. (1992, September 27). Lines drawn in Oregon gay rights battle. *Washington Post*, p. 21.

Zeman, N., & Meyer, R. (1992, November 23). No "special rights" for gays. *Newsweek*, p. 32.

First published May 1993

The World

Our Global Village

We Americans have always had an intense and very complex relationship with the rest of the world. We have moved back and forth between extreme isolation and rather grandiose visions of saving the world for democracy, from hunger, and from other equally grandiose powers with different political and economic interests.

Our responses to other nations and peoples of the world have been shaped by many things: the once wide oceans that both distanced and protected us, the effort to develop our independent nationhood, our need to separate and differentiate ourselves from the Old World, and our desire to construct an identity. Perhaps most important, our relationship with other nations has been shaped by the fact that, with the exception of American Indians, all Americans arrived here fairly recently from other countries or have ancestors who arrived here recently, as time is measured in the history of human events. Thus, we have always had to deal with the diversity of the world within ourselves and within our neighbors.

We have been enormously inconsistent in dealing with potential and actual newcomers. While the Statue of Liberty beckons with a torch of welcome, we have enacted restrictive and racist immigration laws and subjected each wave of new Americans to discrimination, exploitation, and extreme pressure to assimilate to cultural patterns established by the earlier newcomers. In recent decades, our relationship with the rest of the world has been dominated by and organized around our fear of the Soviet Union. This fear has been used to justify occasional military excursions that attempt to protect our economic and ideological hegemony and growing militarism and the stockpiling of enough nuclear weapons to destroy all life on the planet.

At the same time, since the end of the Vietnam War we have seen a new kind of isolationism emerging among many Americans that has developed out of cynicism, growing disen- chantment with our military and political influence in the des- tinies of other people, and a sense of hopelessness about our abili- ty as a nation to save the world from anything. Many of us, faced with the enormous unsolved problems of society, have lost the confidence that we have much of use to offer. Perhaps a new- found humility can be the first step in developing a new kind of relationship with the other peoples of the world.

The social work profession has, of course, reflected these complex social, political, and ideological contexts. We social work practitioners have been at the forefront of assimilationist efforts. We have served in wars and taken leadership in the peace and disarmament movements. We have exported social work methods, consultation, and social work education around the globe, sometimes usefully, sometimes inappropriately. We have put a regrettably small part of our professional energy and resources into international concerns and into collaboration with international social work organizations. With few exceptions, we have been almost completely "Amerocentric" in social work education.

But it is a new world, a different world, a world that demands new responses and major changes on the international, national, professional, and personal levels. First, our protecting oceans have been shrunk by supersonic aircraft, communication satellites, and intercontinental ballistic missiles. In fact, we have come to live, as some have said, in a global village. The earth has become small and the peoples of the world so intimately cross- joined that all of us are deeply affected by events occurring in distant corners of the world, and people in those corners are affected by us. Dramatic examples of the vicious circle of interac- tions include the industrial nations' demanding drug market, the overwhelming debt developing countries owe to industrialized countries, pressure for debt repayment, the destruction of rain forests for the production of coca and the generation of income, and the destruction of the atmosphere through the destruction of the rain forests. Economic, social, political, domestic, international, and ecological issues are intricately bound in an ever-escalating, lethal cycle.

Second, the international political world has been revolutionized. The dramatic events in eastern Europe, *glasnost*, the Soviet Union's peace offensive, and the dismantling of the Berlin Wall and the Iron Curtain have ushered in a new era. But what will we do without our old antagonists? How will we organize and develop coherence and cohesion in this enormously diverse nation without an enemy? How will we justify the continued expenditure of a large portion of our national income on national defense? We must ask, "From whom are we defending ourselves?"

Our nation is changing, too. With the passage of the 1976 and 1978 amendments to the Immigration Act, which opened worldwide immigration on a first-come, first-served basis, and of the Refugee Act of 1980, hundreds of thousands of people are entering the United States yearly, mostly from Central and South America and Asia. Many of these are refugees who bring with them painful memories and deep scars left by violence, loss, torture, and extreme oppression.

What should we as social workers and as citizens do in this new world, our global village? First, we must abandon our anomic isolationism and engage with our world and learn about it. But let us engage in a new way, not as experts or out of noblesse oblige, but as colleagues and partners, with a conviction that in the collaborative process, we have much to learn and share. In this issue [July 1990], James Midgley, one among many with a long-standing dedication to international understanding and partnership, explores the possibilities of learning from the Third World [pp. 295–300]. Also in this issue is an article on Poland's social policy and social welfare system, an example of our new relationship with the nations of Eastern Europe [pp. 302–306].

To help us in our quest for enhanced international understanding and collaboration, the National Association of Social Workers (NASW) has embarked on the Child and Family Well-Being Development Education Project to encourage us to learn about conditions in the developing world so that we may understand how these conditions affect us and our profession in the United States. One goal is the exchange of in formation through collaboration with colleagues in developing countries. Ten NASW chapters have developed partnerships with social workers in developing countries. Other current initiatives include the development of a peace curriculum guide and a program to provide technical assistance to Hungary and Poland.

The profession's growing international commitment is also evident in plans being made by NASW and six other national and international social work organizations for "World Assembly 1992: Improving the Social and Human Condition." This major international initiative will sponsor a variety of activities over a four-year period (1990–1993), including the documentation of effective interventions to promote social welfare and social development, the establishment of international networks, and the development and dissemination of materials for the enhancement of knowledge and skills. The highlight of the initiative will be an integrated national and international conference in Washington, DC, in July 1992. The themes of World Assembly 1992 will be the impact of change on families, political economy and development, and human rights and human needs.

We must act as private citizens and through our professional organizations to encourage our leaders to support the goals of worldwide social justice and peace, in foreign policy and in support of the United Nations. We must voice objections when the United States cuts funds to the U.N. Children's Fund at a time when the situation for children in many of the developing countries is desperate. We must ask why, after 10 years, the United States has yet to ratify the U.N. Convention on the Elimination of All Forms of Discrimination against Women. We must protest our government's nonparticipation in the recent signing of the Convention on the Rights of the Child.

In this new era, when the possibility of world peace is perhaps closer than at any time in decades, we must not simply breathe a sigh of relief and feel that the problems of militarism and nuclear threat have disappeared. On the contrary, we must throw our support behind Social Workers for Peace and Nuclear Disarmament and other groups pressing for arms control and the dismantling of the U.S. nuclear arsenal. Now is the time to demand that our national resources be diverted from preparation for war to the support of programs for people—housing, health care, food, education, and the restoration and preservation of our environment. Many have profited from our growing militarization. Many in power will fight any shift in our national priorities. We are already hearing the self-interested prophets of doom proclaiming, "We must keep our guard up and maintain our military strength because the situation is so unstable in Eastern Europe."

We must prepare ourselves to work with the increasingly diverse population in this country and to understand the culture, the needs, and the experiences of the new immigrants and refugees. Happily, we have once again opened our gates to offer permanent settlement to hundreds of thousands of newcomers a year. But that is not enough. We must develop new ways to help these newcomers enter our society while respecting their culture, lifestyles, and values. We must join with others to ensure that this wave of newcomers does not suffer the discrimination and exploitation suffered by previous newcomers. We must enhance our knowledge and skills in working with new Americans. Jon K. Matsuoka contributed in this regard in his article on Vietnamese refugees [pp. 341–345].

Finally, we must share our abundance with the desperately needy people of the world. A review of materials prepared by the NASW Child and Family Well-Being Development Education Project brings home the steadily worsening conditions in the Third World. We must join with others to relieve the suffering and to support people-centered development in these lands. With changing priorities, we can afford it—the cost of immunization in the developing world is approximately $500 million per year, about the same as the cost of 10 F-14 fighter aircraft.

In the words of the late Daniel Sanders, dean of the University of Illinois, Urbana–Champaign, School of Social Work, who offered such outstanding leadership in the service of world peace and social justice,

> The only lasting peace is a just peace based on respect for human rights and mutuality in relationships. . . . Social work, along with other disci-

plines, has the potential of contributing to shaping the development of a social vision and a new social ethic that will foster respect for life, appreciation of diversity, cultural pluralism, justice in human affairs, participation of people in their own development, and peace. (Staff, 1990, p. 1)

Reference

Staff. (1990, Spring). In Memoriam. *University of Illinois School of Social Work at Urbana–Champaign Newsletter*, p. 1.

First published July 1990

War Stories

January 22, 1991—For the past 48 hours the American people have sat glued to their television sets watching our nation go to war. Although another editorial was planned for this space and although by the time the readers receive this journal the observations that follow will be totally outdated, I feel compelled to reflect on the past 48 hours and on a few of the implications of these momentous events for our profession.

On January 17, 1991, as Americans watched the evening news, ate dinner, drove home, or completed a day at work, the word came that war had begun. Many Americans undoubtedly did not want war. It is likely that many social workers and others, including top military and economic analysts and experts on the Middle East, felt that the United States should have given the economic sanctions more time to work. But now that seemed irrelevant. The die was cast. We were at war.

Watching the beginning of the war on television was such a profound experience for me; the images, the stories, and the sounds replay in my mind and demand examination and reexamination. What messages were being communicated? How was the narrative developing? Watching television that first night was a bizarre experience—intensely intimate on the one hand and coldly distant on the other. The billowing explosions in Baghdad and the roar of planes taking off and returning seemed incredibly close. This was war, brought to us live via satellite.

Anyone who remembers sitting by the radio listening to the static-filled and distorted shortwave broadcast from England in September 1939 that described the beginning of World War II is acutely aware of how communication technology has dissolved distance. One of the most dramatic examples of this was perhaps our view, via cameras mounted on planes, of precisely aimed bombs making direct hits on targets identified by crossed lines.

But at the same time, the experience was distant, surreal. It was almost like watching an electronic video game. The events seemed nonhuman. It was as if machines were fighting machines and technology was fighting technology, but our machines were bigger and better, and our technology was more sophisticated. Bombs dropped on "buildings," "military installations," and "communication centers." These were simply structures. There was no sense that there were human beings in those buildings operating those centers or even that there were human beings guiding our planes. As an officer on a naval vessel that launched the first cruise missiles commented, "They can't see us and we can't see them." This new war provided dramatic contrast to the overwhelmingly intimate face-to-face human struggle pictured in the recent public television series on the Civil War. There, we saw blood, pain, death—the vulnerability of human beings; in this war we see excitement, competition, arrogance, an elaborate game of strategic moves. In the initial hours, military commentators failed to suppress their glee as some of the modern war machinery was tested for the first time and performed with devastating precision.

In the many hours of broadcasts, I saw three poignantly human moments, instant snapshots that stood out. One occurred early on when a television reporter at one of the major airfields in Saudi Arabia became flustered and obviously fearful when the first air-raid sirens sounded. Another was the glimpse of a tearful member of a ground crew watching his plane head for Iraq. The third, shown on the morning of day two, was of a group of lively and smiling Iraqis, including many women and children, singing in an air-raid shelter. Although most film segments were shown repeatedly, I saw this one only once. It is dangerous to see the humanness of our enemy. It might undermine our resolve.

How can we understand these momentous happenings? What do they mean? Meaning arises out of the interaction between an event and the interpretation of that event and is formulated and reformulated over time. The events in the Persian Gulf are mediated by television news reporters, expert commentators, carefully prepared military personnel, and political leaders. In turn, as we take in these mediated versions of the war, we create our own meanings to be tested and reshaped in our meaning-making contexts. As we watch the political leaders of every country involved, the families of service women and men, and the antiwar protesters, these events take on a different meaning as alternate narratives are developed by those in different contexts, and we begin to construct the meaning of what is romantically called "Operation Desert Storm."

A fascinating example of this meaning-formulation process can be found in President George Bush's choice of language as he spoke to the nation that first night. He began with, "The liberation of Kuwait has begun," much like Dwight D. Eisenhower when he announced World War II's D-Day landings in Normandy with, "The liberation of Europe is under way." This use of similar language was an attempt to link Operation Desert Storm with our last "good" war, a war memorialized as both moral and victorious. Another example of this linkage was Bush's referring to the multinational armies as "the allied forces."

This new war has multiple meanings, many of which compete. However, the narratives, the definitions, and the interpretations promoted by those in power tend to become dominant, shaping the discourse and assuming the garb of truth. The dominant narrative emerged couched in language that sanitizes the events and helps us deny the human agony. Such terms as "clean surgical strikes" communicate a bloodless intervention. "Collateral damage" obliquely refers to the destruction of people and property that are not military targets.

But there is another story about the war, another kind of language that is rarely heard. This subjugated language is the language of pain, blood, misery, and death. It is the story of what is happening to human beings on both sides of this conflict. It is dangerous language; it makes the horror of war real. It is the kind of story that is usually told long after a war, as in the motion pictures *Platoon, Born on the Fourth of July,* and *Glory.*

The discourse of powerful people is dominant not only because their words carry the weight of their prestige, but also because they can use their power to control access to information. At this early point in the war, there is strong concern among the media that access to information is being controlled by the Pentagon not only to meet the demands of military security, but also to present a picture of the war constructed to maintain public support and to maintain the dominant narrative. Our government learned some lessons in Vietnam. One was that the open, intimate, and horrifying picture of the Vietnam struggle presented by the press had enormous political impact and was a major factor in fueling the antiwar movement. Who can forget the widely printed news photo of Vietnamese children, on fire from a napalm attack, running toward the camera?

At this stage in the gulf war, all news correspondents must travel in groups accompanied by an information officer; all stories, pictures, and news footage are reviewed by security officers. Although the military insists that this is an effort to facilitate reporting, newspeople argue that it seriously interferes with their ability to gather information and communicate it to the public. As one reporter asked, "How is a soldier going to be able to really talk while a military information officer is looking over his shoulder?" This is the subtle process of the suppression of personal, private knowledge.

What does the war mean to and for us as citizens and as social workers? How can we respond? I have been struggling with this question since the war began and can only share my initial thoughts. My first reaction and the reaction of many others, I am sure, was an overwhelming feeling of helplessness. We are all involved in momentous events over which we have little control. Fairly quickly, as our mechanized might seemed so successful in the early hours of the war, I found to my horror that my sense of helplessness was momentarily relieved as I identified with American military power. Our team was winning and the excitement was catching. But that was not the way I wanted to become empowered. What can we do? How can we convert helplessness into action? At this early stage of the war, this is my own initial agenda.

First, as social workers, it is often our role to connect the political and personal, to articulate the impact that political decisions and socioeconomic conditions have on people, and to expose the pain and vulnerability in human experience. All of us in our public positions and in private conversations can challenge the evolving dominant discourse on this war. We must continue to bring forth the human story and to insist that the public receive information about what is happening to real people. We must join with the media in their outrage over censorship. We must do our best to hang on to and talk about war's human realities. The dissemination of this kind of information can have an impact on how the war is waged and on when and how it ends.

Second, with our expertise in the human side of war, we must be available to work with the families of service men and women as they face separation, abiding fear, and loss. We also should prepare ourselves to meet the needs of returning soldiers. We have learned from Vietnam how to be more fully and quickly responsive to the psychological and social impact of the war experience. Although the military has not wanted this known, it is estimated that the conditions of this war will produce a higher incidence of psychiatric casualties than in any previous war. We must be ready to help these survivors and their families. We have learned how the Vietnam War continues to affect veterans and their families years after the American withdrawal. Perhaps we can help prevent these long-lasting reverberations for those involved in Operation Desert Storm.

Finally, we must actively work for peace. Perhaps the one positive aspect of this war is that most of the world's nations have joined in a common cause. With all of the major powers on the same side, we may have a chance to build a lasting peace. We must not squander this opportunity.

First published March 1991

The Nation

Good Luck, Bill–Keep in Touch

This month, Bill and Hillary Rodham Clinton move into the White House, marking the end of an increasingly conservative Republican rule that began in 1968, interrupted only briefly by the Carter administration in 1976. The Clintons come to Washington bringing the youth, intelligence, charm, and energy that is reminiscent of the excitement of John F. Kennedy's "Camelot."

The Clinton–Gore victory has generated for many Americans a domestic version of Operation Restore Hope, as spirits have been lifted by the possibility of change, by the possibility that we will once again turn our attention to the overwhelming problems that face American society. And it is important that we feel hopeful; hope generates energy, ideas, solutions, investment, and sacrifices for the common good and for a future that has meaning.

But with the excitement and the hope have come heightened and often unrealistic expectations. Probably typical was one automobile worker, a "Reagan Democrat" interviewed on television right after the election, who said, "I'll give him one year!" Such unrealistic views of how long it is going to take to reweave the tattered fabric of our society, to reverse the powerful negative economic processes, and to rehabilitate our nation after years of neglect will undermine hope and trust. Such expectations can lead only to disappointment and disillusionment.

Perhaps the most important change that must take place is in the American people's vision of government and of the social contract on which that government rests. The relationship between the government and the people must include mutual trust and responsibility. Both have been increasingly irresponsible and distrustful. The government has been irresponsibly neglectful, but the people have adopted the position that we can have it all and not pay for it. This view, of course, has been encouraged by the Republican antitax rhetoric. The American people, as individuals and as a collective, have been living on borrowed money and must face the fact that now we must pay the piper. We must reduce the deficit, we must reduce the debt, and we must increase our investment in our social institutions, in our people, and in our physical environment. We need tax reform; we need to redistribute the tax burden so that those people with higher incomes carry a greater share, but middle-income people must also pay more. The American people currently pay the lowest taxes by far of any industrialized nation.

But the American people don't want to pay taxes, not only because they want to protect their resources, but also because they do not trust the government to use those resources wisely, carefully, and for the common good. Not only do many people object to the extent to which our resources have been spent on military might, but they also object to the graft and corruption, waste, and duplication, and financial disasters such as the savings and loan scandal. One of the greatest challenges facing the Clinton administration and the new Congress will be to rekindle Americans' trust in government so Americans will be more willing to shoulder their responsibilities in this partnership.

A second challenge faced by President-elect Clinton will be to build a government that represents and is sensitive to and knowledgeable about the diversity in American society. The leadership in past administrations did not mirror the American people, and the great social distance that has existed between those in government and those governed has also bred suspicion and distrust. This distance was most dramatically demonstrated when Anita Hill faced the all-white–male Senate Judiciary Committee in the Hill–Thomas hearings. After all the progress made in the 1960s and 1970s, we have witnessed a growing backlash of sexism, racism, and homophobia. Evidence of that backlash can be found across the nation—in inner cities, in the workplace, and on college campuses. The lack of concern at the highest levels of government about issues of diversity in this country has given subtle permission for the most ugly and hateful discriminatory attitudes to rise to the surface, to be spoken and enacted, and to be tolerated.

The new Congress and the new Senate look a little more like the American people, and President-elect Clinton has made clear his intention to build a government that includes more than just a token number of women and members of ethnic and racial minorities in key positions. His history of working collaboratively and productively with diverse populations in Arkansas and his willingness to support the rights of gay men and lesbians to serve in the armed forces speak to his sensitivity to issues of diversity. We must demonstrate to ourselves and to the world that a diverse people can live together in harmony, can respect and even celebrate difference at the same time that they reach across those differences to join in common cause. The actions of our leaders in this regard have tremendous influence on the norms, the values, and the behaviors of the entire nation.

A third major challenge of the new administration is to navigate among the powerful lobbies and special-interest groups that have formed a barrier between the government and the nation as a whole. President-elect Clinton's agenda includes many issues that will directly counter the interests of some of the most powerful lobbies in Washington. Health care reform moves directly into the territory of the insurance lobby and the American Medical Association. Any approach to the problem of violence in this country must include gun control and a direct assault on the power of the National Rifle Association.

The dilemma is complex. The new administration needs eight years to make real headway in rebuilding, and to do the job, the special-interest groups must be challenged. Such challenges threaten the possibility of a second term. This dilemma will call on all the administration's collaborative and negotiating skills.

Finally, as the enormous administrative and bureaucratic structure, as the pomp and panoply, and as the security forces close in around Clinton on Inauguration Day, how can he maintain a connection with the American people? How can he keep from being distanced, from being increasingly isolated behind these barricades? It is possible that President George Bush didn't lose the election because of the economy but rather because he was out of touch with the American people and they knew it. His distance from the stresses, from the economic insecurity, from the plight of the average American was shockingly evident throughout the campaign and was particularly demonstrated in the presidential debate where he was face-to-face with the voters. It might be said that he had a helicopter's-eye view of the daily life of the American people.

President-elect Clinton clearly enjoys people—all kinds of people. He was frequently late on the campaign trail because he was always stopping to talk with people. He seems determined to stay in touch. The economic summit in Arkansas in December, part show business and part problem exploration, not only included the public through television, but also involved people at the grassroots level in the conversation. He promises other public forums. President-elect Clinton also must get out to where the people are not only to communicate to them that he is available and concerned, but also to gain some firsthand knowledge of the lives of his constituency.

But time and safety will not allow for much of that. We would not want him to slip away from his guards, as Abraham Lincoln did, and walk through the streets of Washington alone. But there are ways of staying in touch. Franklin D. Roosevelt, who was wheelchair bound, kept in touch through Eleanor Roosevelt, who traveled as an intelligent and empathic observer all over the country and brought him faithful and vital reports on poor people, children, unemployed workers, and victims of disasters. The newspaper picture of her descending into a mine shaft to gain a greater sense of the lives of miners was memorable and typical.

President-elect Clinton needs several peripatetic, sensitive, and committed observer–reporters who can bring him information and not be afraid to tell him the bad news as well as the good. He also needs to stay in close touch with the people in his administration. For example, it has been suggested that he not appoint a chief of staff to avoid placing someone between himself and his major advisors and administrators. Chiefs of staff have protected the president, but such protection can prevent the president from knowing what he ought to know and from dealing directly with people.

And, perhaps to reduce the distance between himself and those who put him in office, President-elect Clinton can limit the formal regalia and ritual that has grown up recently around the presidency. The almost regal pageantry does not seem appropriate for a democratic republic and again creates awe and separates the citizens and their citizen president. The power of the presidential role is seductive, but perhaps this Arkansan can do what Jimmy Carter did and end the trumpeting of "Hail to the Chief!"

Good luck, Bill. Keep in touch.

First published January 1993

Writing a New Story
about America

In November 1992, the American public, whether supporting Clinton or Perot, voted overwhelmingly for change. Americans were moved by many disappointments, frustrations, and angers: unemployed workers by the hopelessness of their situation; poor people by the steady decline in resources available to them; women by the erosion of reproductive rights and by the fact that their powerlessness has not been appreciably redressed, particularly in the political arena; working- and middle-class people by the deterioration of the quality of their lives and the steady shift of resources to the wealthier segments of society; and others by the steady deterioration of our institutions and national infrastructure. Many Americans were moved by the shadow of the deficit, which is escalating every year and mortgaging the future of our children and our children's children. Furthermore, many Americans were increasingly suspicious of a government that seems to operate behind closed doors, protected from observation and accountability.

In recent years, the stories of America have been in Michael White's (1989) words—problem-saturated stories of decaying institutions, of violence and drugs, of escalating poverty, of a failing economy, and of seemingly irreversible deindustrialization. Furthermore, American leadership has tried to counteract these problem-saturated narratives with denial and cheerful predictions. But denial and cheerfulness ceased to satisfy the American public; they wanted change.

President Bill Clinton offered in his economic address to a joint session of the Congress and to the American people an economic and social plan that is intended to dramatically change the direction and alter the shape of American public policy, to reverse Reaganomics, and to end 12 years of social laissez-faire.

The outline of the economic and social plan is well known. Major provisions are to redistribute income and resources to begin to combat inequality; to sharply cut military spending; to selectively reduce the size of the federal bureaucracy; to increase taxes for middle- and upper-income families, with people in the higher brackets shouldering more of the burden; to create jobs; to support small business; and to reduce the federal deficit.

President Clinton has responded to the mandate for change by offering a program that analyst Robert Pear (1993) called "a blueprint for one of the most profound changes in social policy in this century" (p. 3). At this writing, we are awaiting the plans for the reform of the health care system and support for education. Although Clinton has been fairly quiet to date on education (with the exception of Head Start, job training, and forgiveness of college loans through public service), his record as governor of Arkansas would predict future attention to this crucial area.

President Clinton has also offered a counterchallenge to the American people to participate in this change and to contribute their fair share. He has challenged the "me first" attitude and the greed that have been a part of the American story and that have been exaggerated in recent years. It is noteworthy that the position presented by the Republican leader of the House of Representatives immediately after Clinton's address was one of again appealing to people's concern with their pocketbooks, with dire predictions made about what sacrifices might be asked of them.

Will Americans rise to Clinton's challenge? Will we join with the president and his team to construct new stories for America, stories full of promise and possibilities?

In the depths of the Great Depression, President Franklin D. Roosevelt, in an effort to rouse a devastated America, warned of the power of fear as a self-fulfilling prophecy. Now, as then, what would hold us back are problem-filled narratives about our country, narratives of cynicism, hopelessness, and despair.

The immediate response of the American people to President Clinton was moving and encouraging as almost without exception, people from all parts of society said they were willing to do their fair share. Will this positive response be sustained through the long haul? It will take a long time to put things right in America.

American history embodies two conflicting ideological heritages that have characterized political, economic, and social life. One is the strong individualistic tradition that treasures human rights such as privacy, speech, religion, and also property rights and the right to bear arms. A second tradition, which has struggled less successfully for expression, is concern for the common good, for the welfare of community and society. The United States has lagged far behind most European industrialized nations in its willingness to commit resources and energies to the welfare of all. "Buried deep in our rights dialect is an unexpressed premise that we roam at large in a land of strangers, where we presumptively have no obligations toward others except to avoid the actual infliction of harm" (Glendon, 1991, p. 77). Too often devotion to individual rights neglects the "social dimensions of human personhood" (p. 109).

It has been primarily in times of war that Americans have submerged individual rights and their differences and willingly sacrificed for the national welfare. Those who are old enough to have lived through World War II remember the strong sense of shared purpose, of willingness to contribute in hundreds of ways to what became a total and single-minded effort. World War II was a painful and difficult time, but it was a time when Americans felt good about themselves as a nation and a people. President John F. Kennedy tried and was partially successful in stirring a commitment to social good, but Camelot and the country's aspirations for a Great Society foundered on the violence of assassination and the bitter divisiveness and disillusionment of Vietnam.

Even in peacetime, the threat of the ever-present Evil Empire has been used to stimulate national cohesiveness and rationalize the enormous sacrifice the nation has made in diverting so much of our national wealth to military buildup.

With the evaporation of the Russian threat and the growing diversity of the nation, what common cause can enable Americans to find shared goals within our differences and build a nation that protects essential human rights and is also committed to the common good? Can we come together to build a just society, a strong economy, and a true democracy where both the necessities of life and opportunities are available to all? President Clinton has challenged the American people to write a new American story filled with options and opportunity.

How is this new story being created? American leadership is also currently undergoing a revolution in style. President Clinton is constructing a new narrative about the nation out of an amazingly open process in which he is a direct participant. He is continuing an ongoing conversation with a large and varied group of advisors who seem to have endless energy. He is also in a conversation with the American people. Although his travels around the country have been disparaged as commercial salesmanship, his efforts to reach the American people and gain their support seem to be working. Without clear and vocal public approval, a cautious Congress, anxiously anticipating the next election, will probably be afraid to support a program that asks the American public to give more, to contribute, to put aside short-term self-interest to turn the nation around.

President Clinton is asking for our support, and it is important that all of us who share his aspirations and are willing to participate in their advancement let it be known to him and to our representatives in Congress. We have been challenged and in the end it is up to us to continue the conversation and to help write a new story about America.

References

Glendon, M. A. (1991). *Rights talk: The impoverishment of political discourse*. New York: Free Press.

Pear, R. (1993, February 21). Clean break: Clinton's bold plan sets social policy his way. *New York Times*, pp. 1, 3, Section 4.

White, M. (1989). *Selected papers*. South Australia: Dulwich Center Publications.

First published March 1993

Social Policy

Homelessness: Public Issue and Private Trouble

In this enormously wealthy country, homelessness is a national disgrace. It is a metaphor and a symptom—a metaphor for an irresponsible and careless society, a symptom that something is very wrong in the land of the free and the home of the brave.

The existence of homelessness provokes a variety of responses: anger, outrage, guilt, shame, and perhaps most devastating, an overwhelming sense of helplessness. Social workers have dealt with homelessness in a variety of ways. Some have taken action by trying to alleviate the effects of homelessness on individuals and families and by locating and delivering services, either through paid work or through volunteer effort.

Many of us, however, when faced with such a painful situation and a sense of helplessness, look the other way. We deny, we minimize. We even are beginning to get used to homelessness. We are beginning to consider the existence of a homeless population an inevitable part of our society. We step around the piles of rags on ventilating shaft grates, averting our eyes, not wanting to know that under those rags is a human being.

We read of the increasing number of families, mothers and children, and elderly people without shelter or homes, and our capacity for empathy fails us. We begin to distance ourselves from these people; we begin to think of them as a faceless group—"the homeless." We begin to think of homelessness as a personal characteristic rather than a tragic situation in which people find themselves. We reframe a public issue, everyone's issue, as primarily a private trouble.

Our imagination also fails us. We find it hard to grasp what it would be like to have no place, no piece of territory that, no matter how modest, is home. We study the mental health of homeless people and find them severely troubled. For example, in one study (Hagen & Ivanoff, 1988), a group of homeless women were interviewed and tested through a self-administered symptom checklist. The women reported a range of symptoms: nervousness, low energy, annoyance or irritation, and loneliness. Many felt confused, worried, and were "stewing about things" and blaming themselves. They experienced hurt feelings and wanted to be alone. An analysis of the data revealed that "the women's interpersonal sensitivity and depression scores . . . were at or above the clinical norm for depressed and anxious psychiatric outpatients" (p. 31) and the mean scores on somatization, obsessive-compulsiveness, and anxiety were more than one standard deviation higher than the norms for a general, nonclinical population.

How may we understand these findings? How can they be interpreted? Can we stretch our imaginations? Could it be that homelessness creates feelings of depression, anxiety, and interpersonal sensitivity? Is it strange that a person would experience depression in the face of such loss, and experience anxiety in response to insecurity and danger? Is it odd that people living in a congregate situation desire solitude or that interpersonal sensitivity develops when there is so little privacy?

Public policy has tended to link homelessness and mental illness. For example, the major federal response to homelessness has been the Stewart B. McKinney Homeless Assistance Act of 1987. Although any positive response to the problem of homelessness is welcome, the focus of this legislation is entirely residual. The McKinney Act encourages the delivery of needed mental health and shelter services, but not permanent housing. Research and demonstration projects provided for through the McKinney Act focus on homeless people who suffer from alcoholism, other drug addictions, or mental illness. The national Resource Center on Homelessness and Mental Illness also has been established. These approaches are important and useful, but they define homelessness in terms of private troubles.

How else can we understand the fact that there are approximately 3 million homeless people in the United States (Kozol, 1988)? Homelessness is a result of the steady disappearance and unavailability of low-cost housing. Thousands of housing units are lost every year through gentrification, "urban renewal," decay, and fire. As a matter of public policy, these units are not replaced. Under the Reagan administration, the federal government cut support for new low-income housing by 76 percent (Reamer, 1989), and we have recently learned of the abuse and mismanagement of the remaining funds administered by the U.S. Department of Housing and Urban Development. When an essential commodity is scarce, competition for it intensifies and the most vulnerable lose; those with the fewest resources have the least power.

The resources available to these vulnerable populations have decreased as the real value of public assistance payments has declined and social programs have been decimated. Clearly, the so-called "safety net" is full of holes, and the homeless have fallen through.

Homelessness also is related to deinstitutionalization, a program born in the idealism of an earlier time but now undermined and subverted. Deinstitutionalization was part of a progressive public policy, sparked by the rights movements and enunciated in the 1960s and 1970s, which stated that children, people who were mentally ill or developmentally disabled, and other populations with special needs should be cared for in the "least restrictive environment." As the least restrictive principle was translated into programs, people who were chronically mentally ill were moved back into the community. Under a more socially responsible administration, institutions would have been replaced by a range of supportive community aftercare services planned to maintain and protect marginally functional people in less-restrictive environments. However, as the political and social direction of the nation changed, aftercare and community services never were established or were cut, and the least restrictive environment became an alienating and unresponsive place with no protection, no support, no services, and for many, no homes. The primary response to the crisis of homelessness has been the ad hoc development of shelters, soup kitchens, and other forms of temporary provision through public and voluntary efforts. Those who have worked to make these emergency services available, often against great odds, are to be commended.

However, in some respects, shelters are reminiscent of the birthplaces of social welfare efforts. They seem to be latter-day versions of the late-18th- and 19th-century poorhouses that provided shelter for people who were displaced, poor, or mentally or physically ill. In fact, the history of social welfare policy and service development has been a gradual effort to separate the varied populations in need of care and to develop and offer differential responses through an individualizing process. It is almost as if the profession were back where it started, and social workers are bearing witness, as did our professional ancestors. They are gathering information on those who are homeless and reporting that the homeless population must be differentiated and individualized, that different groups of homeless people need different kinds of services and resources.

Social workers are bearing witness in the pages of this journal [November 1989]. We learn more about homeless women and families in Detroit and in St. Louis. We learn that within this group, a range of services are required. But as we gather information about individuals' private troubles, care must be taken that we never forget the public issues that frame these private troubles. For example, a new typology is becoming part of the discourse on the homeless. This typology includes four categories of homeless people: (1) the situationally homeless, (2) the chronically mentally ill, (3) alcoholics, and (4) street people (Breaky & Fischer, 1985; Sullivan & Damrosch, 1986). Are we falling into the old trap of separating the worthy from the unworthy poor, of identifying one group as homeless "through no fault of their own"? People who are chronically mentally ill also are situationally homeless, the situation being created by the emptying of the mental hospitals without substitute programs for housing, support, and care being in place.

The profession must, of course, go beyond bearing witness. We must be on the line with homeless people to reach out and offer help in the face of overwhelming private troubles. In Marcia B. Cohen's "Social Work Practice with Homeless Mentally Ill People" [pp. 505–509] and Barbara Parmer Davidson and Pamela J. Jenskin's "Class Diversity in Shelter Life" [pp. 491–495], particular knowledge and skills required to work with two very different homeless populations are presented. Our profession also must take leadership in developing creative and innovative demonstration and research projects, such as the one described in Nancy M. Kroloff and Sandra C. Anderson's "Alcohol-free Living Centers: Hope for Homeless Alcoholics" [pp. 497–504].

But bearing witness, attempting to ameliorate private troubles, and setting up innovative helping programs are not enough. We must be clear that homelessness cannot be reduced appreciably by treating individual troubles. The problem of homelessness is a public issue and can be resolved only through public action and major changes in public policy. Poverty must be reduced and low-cost housing must be made available. This effort, of course, requires a major reordering of our national agenda. It requires a major investment in the welfare of the nation's vulnerable citizens. It demands the rebuilding and expansion of social programs and the recognition that economic resources do not "trickle down" but must be redistributed through public consensus. This year [1989], the National Association of Social Workers chose the problem of homelessness as its public service campaign theme. An extensive and effective educational program has been focused on raising public awareness of and concern about the problem of homelessness.

But education also is not enough. We must join with others to bring about a change in public policy. We must advocate on national, state, and local levels and demand from our legislatures a response to what perhaps should be reframed as "the housing crisis." We must resist the ever-present pressure to redefine this public issue, this public disgrace.

References

Breaky, W. R., & Fischer, P. J. (1985, June). Down and out in the land of plenty. *Johns Hopkins Magazine*, pp. 16–24.

Hagen, J. L., & Ivanoff, A. M. (1988). Homeless women: A high-risk population. *Affilia: Journal of Women and Social Work, 3*, 19–33.

Kozol, J. (1988, January). A reporter at large: The homeless and their children. *New Yorker*, pp. 65–84.

Reamer, F. G. (1989). The affordable housing crisis and social work. *Social Work, 34,* 5–9.

Stewart B. McKinney Homeless Assistance Act of 1987, P.L. 100-77, 101 Stat. 482.

Sullivan, P. A., & Damrosch, S. P. (1986). Homeless women and children. In R. D. Bingham, R. E. Green, & S. B. White (Eds.), *The homeless in contemporary society* (pp. 82–98). Newbury Park, CA: Sage Publications.

First published November 1989

Where Do We Go from Here?

Caitlin C. Ryan

For two weeks this summer, I had the opportunity to remove myself from a typical task-driven day and focus on the future. I was asked to represent the National Association of Social Workers (NASW) before the National Commission on AIDS as it considered personnel and work force issues. The issue I was asked to address—how social work recruitment and retention have been affected by the acquired immune deficiency syndrome (AIDS) epidemic—required a review of how we plan and implement future policies that affect our profession. In preparation for the hearing, I interviewed social workers from across the country: line workers, students, faculty, deans, supervisors, hospital social work directors, clients, and some I consider to be social work visionaries. Not all worked in AIDS-related fields, but all were affected by the additional burden the AIDS epidemic has placed on health, mental health, and social services agencies, and all were deeply concerned about the future of the social work profession. Their responses were provocative and disturbing.

I tapped into a wellspring of anxiety, frustration, and apprehension. Social workers on the front line of AIDS care, agency and hospital social work directors, social workers with smaller AIDS caseloads in low-incidence states, social workers who work with AIDS patients in areas heavily affected by AIDS, and social work educators all shared common feelings and concerns. They spoke of their fear of the future, increasing frustration over mounting caseloads, and anxiety regarding cutbacks in services. Many shared feelings of alienation and anger, concerns about posttraumatic stress, and trepidation over facing the growing pressure of another decade of human services under siege.

All considered similar questions. What will the future be like for social work and AIDS in five to 10 years? What competing social concerns will make it more difficult to meet the needs of people infected with and at risk for human immunodeficiency virus (HIV) infection? What would it be like if social workers were not there? How can we recruit and retain committed young workers, including minorities, into a profession characterized by a poor public image, low prestige, and low pay? Are we adequately preparing students and practitioners for an aging and multicultural society where individuals and families will have even less access to support from traditional social institutions?

Hardly anyone could anticipate the future; most were struggling with the present. However, considering the growing caseloads of people with HIV disease, the soaring costs of health care, and cutbacks in state and local programs, their reports were grim. This is what they said:

• There currently are not enough trained social workers to provide essential services in many parts of the country, not just for people with AIDS but for other areas of practice as well. In especially short supply are minority, bilingual and bicultural, and AIDS social workers.

• Overall, social workers lack sufficient AIDS training; specific training on substance use, including identification and treatment of chemically dependent clients; training in managing chronic illness; and training in providing primary prevention services to meet the needs of patients. Many social workers are still fearful and uncomfortable with people who have AIDS.

• Few agencies have adapted policies to manage the high stress and grief overload associated with providing care to people with AIDS, thus contributing to the burnout of social workers who remain in those settings. Most agencies still fail to provide support groups for workers. They enforce rigid policies that do not take into account the special needs of physically debilitated, multiproblem clients and require workers to juggle large mixed caseloads, when AIDS patients alone require additional services and counseling.

• Social workers in community agencies feel overburdened by breakdowns in other systems, particularly public hospitals and public social services agencies. These problems ultimately interfere with the social worker's ability to provide appropriate or even minimal care to people with AIDS. In particular, there are insufficient mental health and psychiatric day treatment programs available to meet the mounting demands related to AIDS.

• Traditionally high burnout areas, such as child abuse and adolescent services, are especially affected by the AIDS epidemic. Workers in high-incidence areas are struggling to help children manage bereavement. In New York City, at least 10,000 children have already lost one or both parents to AIDS; some have lost as many as 13 or 14 relatives. Social workers cannot find the resources needed to help these children, often because such resources and services are unavailable.

• Social work students are turning away from hospital social work and AIDS-related social work, particularly in high-incidence areas where a larger selection of practicum placements is available. The multiproblem, overlapping vulnerabilities of newer populations of AIDS patients overwhelm many social workers and discourage them from entering or staying in AIDS care, particularly when there is insufficient support and inadequate supervision.

Given so many pressing concerns, most social workers feel powerless and overwhelmed when asked about the future. The failure of the social work profession to respond early to the AIDS crisis (reflecting the failure of the larger society to do so) short-circuited any opportunity to prepare for the chaos that would follow. During the past five years, AIDS has been touted as providing an opportunity to address long-standing systemic health and social problems. However, a business-as-usual attitude, more talk than action, and a reluctance to take risks have characterized most institutional responses.

What does this say about our capacity or responsibility to plan for the future or to shift our priorities when crisis occurs? How do we plan ahead? Beyond updating and adopting policy statements and goals at the Delegate Assembly every few years, what augurs do we follow and how are they read? Who are our forecasters and what must happen before we listen to them?

We are somewhere in the midst of the AIDS epidemic right now. Considering the vulnerability of those at risk for and affected by AIDS, social work, as a profession, has been scandalously slow to act. In addition to failing to provide leadership and practice guidelines during earlier stages of the epidemic, we are the only major national professional association that has not instituted an official policy advisory group on AIDS. We are the only one of three major national associations representing mental health professionals (the other two are the American Psychological Association and the American Psychiatric Association) that has not implemented a professional training program for its members. Yet we are the only major professional association with an ethical mandate to serve the poor and oppressed.

The social work profession is a critical and as yet untapped resource in the international struggle to meet the challenges of AIDS. As a profession, we must call on our leaders, our teachers, and certainly our members to quickly and decisively take the following six critical steps:

1. Social work schools must reallocate resources to integrate and add vital curriculum components to prepare new workers to face the demands of practice during the AIDS epidemic.

2. Schools of social work must work intensively within their communities to develop incentives for students to select AIDS-related practicum placements.

3. NASW, together with schools of social work, must demonstrate an unprecedented level of cooperation in developing and disseminating low-cost postgraduate training for students and stress-reduction networks for social workers already overwhelmed by the multiproblem nature of AIDS.

4. NASW must work with major agency coalitions to develop and promulgate standards for agency policies that respond to the multiple needs of HIV-infected people, their families, and caregivers.

5. NASW must spearhead a coalition to work with federal agencies and state and local governments to address the demand for critical community services and growing resource gaps.

6. NASW must advertise publicly and definitively the crucial need for a coordinated social work response to the AIDS epidemic and must actively support the key contribution individual practitioners continue to make.

If we take these steps, social work as a profession will make enormous strides in healing the massive social disruption and pain brought about by the AIDS epidemic. If we view this catastrophe as a test of our ability to plan, react, and rapidly reassign priorities, we could learn a great deal. Then perhaps during the next major social crisis, social work could lead the way.

Caitlin C. Ryan, MSW, ACSW, has worked in the AIDS epidemic for 11 years. Correspondence should be sent to 33 Adams Street, NW, Washington, DC 20001.

First published January 1991

Toward a Redefinition and Recontextualization of the Abortion Issue

Our nation is involved in an enormously painful and intense struggle: the struggle over legal abortion. The legalization of abortion by the Supreme Court in 1973 through *Roe v. Wade* did not resolve the issue. On the contrary, the conflict has steadily escalated. We are now facing a possible reconsideration of *Roe v. Wade* by a conservative Reagan–Bush Court with the real possibility that the earlier decision will be overturned.

As abortion increasingly becomes a focus of national debate, it is perhaps useful to step back from the fray and think about this crucial issue, about how it has been formulated and shaped. The definition of a problem tends to direct the discourse concerning it and to expand or limit the options and possibilities for solution. Thus, it is useful to examine the definitions of the abortion issue and the implications of these definitions.

In *Roe v. Wade*, the Supreme Court defined the issue as a matter of privacy. This was congruent with the legal tradition that prohibited state interference in the marital relationship. This tradition, of course, has also denied women legal protection from economic and physical abuse by their husbands. Although privacy is an important consideration, this definition by the court buttresses the conservative idea that the personal is separate from the political and that the larger social structure has no impact on private individual choice (Copelon, 1990).

What women really won in *Roe v. Wade* was the right to be left alone. The right to privacy guarantees noninterference but does not guarantee self-determination. Social supports and resources are required for true self-determination. The right to be left alone was made even more complete through the Court's decision on *Harris v. McRae* (1980), which upheld the right of Congress and state legislatures to refuse to pay for abortions for poor women. This trend has continued with the 1991 ruling in *Rust v. Sullivan*, which upholds the government's right to refuse to support the giving of abortion counseling, information, or referral.

Making abortion a woman's prerogative makes it easier to make it a woman's problem.

> Since contraception and abortion are entirely within a woman's control, the argument runs, pregnancy, child-bearing and child-rearing are her responsibility. Extending the right to be left alone to abortion makes it seem legitimate not only for taxpayers, but also for the fathers of unborn children, to leave the freely choosing right-bearer alone. (Glendon, 1991, p. 66)

Thus, the Supreme Court decision, relying as it does on the individual's privacy rights, ignores the context that enables or limits choice. Although *Roe v. Wade* limits the state's right to interfere in the lives of women, it does not limit the intrusion of social conditions that determine options. The legalization of abortion makes it possible for those with information, access, and resources to achieve reproductive choice. Reproductive choice has become a privilege of the economically secure and enormously burdensome or unattainable for those with limited resources. It is understandable that many women of color have not joined in the campaign for choice. Not only does any birth control campaign stir memories of genocide and racist eugenics (Davis, 1990), but many recognize that all that is at stake for them is the right to be left alone.

In the escalating conflict over abortion since *Roe v. Wade*, the privacy issue has been left behind and the struggle has increasingly been defined by activists in terms of a clash of absolute and immutable rights—a deadlock between the fetus's right to life and the woman's right to control her body. The definition of the issue in terms of absolute rights is congruent with American individualistic traditions grounded originally in the Anglo-Saxon sanctification of property rights. However, as

Glendon (1991) has pointed out in her volume *Rights Talk*, this tendency to frame nearly every social controversy in terms of a clash of rights impedes compromise, mutual understanding, and the discovery of common ground. It is the end of dialogue and, as we have seen, the beginning of violence.

Both positions, the right to life and the right to choose, have generated volumes of legalistic arguments that promote the positions convincingly but do not move a step nearer to solution. For example the Reagan administration, in its campaign against abortion, took the "benefit of the doubt" position. One of the cornerstones of Western medical ethics and cultural tradition is that when there is uncertainty as to whether life is present, benefit of the doubt is given as if it were. Applying this to abortion allows those opposed to it to avoid taking a definitive position on the viability of the fetus while giving the fetus the benefit of the doubt (Pfeiffer, 1985).

On the other side, those favoring reproductive rights focus on the rights people have in relation to the control of their bodies. They argue that the right to life does not include the right to another person's body. If this were the case, the argument goes, would it not then imply that denying an organ for transplant to a dying person would be a violation of that person's right to life (Ketchum, 1984)? Such discourse on rights can become increasingly convoluted but does not indicate a way to deal with this crucial conflict in a highly diverse society. Furthermore, rights arguments tend, in their absoluteness, individualism, and insularity, to be silent with respect to personal, civic, and collective responsibility.

Both positions have some built-in inconsistencies that become immediately apparent when one stands back from the rhetoric. For example, those who take such a strong position on a woman's right to control her body must be reminded that the use of abortion also places all of the burden for reproductive choice on that body. Abortion as a fail-safe option because no contraceptive is fully effective is one thing. Use of abortion as a first-line birth control method as so casually expressed in the comment "Don't worry, you can always get an abortion" is another. This misogynist position is found in some highly patriarchal countries where women carry the full burden and many go through multiple abortions.

The absolutist right-to-life position also has extended implications that must be faced by those who take this position. Most important perhaps is the fact that the right to life, if it truly begins at conception, should not end at the moment of birth. The inconsistency of the positions of our "pro-life" federal administration has been dramatic. Although the rights of the unborn have been defended, social and health programs needed to enhance the lives of infants and children have been decimated. If we really care so much about life, about children, how can we allow one in five to live in poverty? How can we tolerate being 19th among the nations in infant mortality? If we believe in the fetus's right to life, why have funds been cut for prenatal care? If we want to protect children, we must make social and economic supports available to their parents. The inconsistency of the "pro-life but against social programs" position is expressed in the number of women who must seek abortion not out of choice, but out of hopelessness or bitter necessity (Copelon, 1990). The inconsistency of many who espouse the right-to-life position is also seen in the fact that "studies have repeatedly shown that people's views on abortion are best predicted by their opinions on sex and family issues, not on 'life' issues like nuclear weapons or the death penalty" (Willis, 1990, p. 138). One is left asking if the concern is really with life or with the changing roles and status of women, with the liberation of women from compulsory motherhood.

Finally, both absolutist positions, focusing as they do on the rights of an individual or a potential individual, are remarkably decontextualized. Both ignore the cultural context. Both are fighting for an absolutist position in a land of diversity of values, beliefs, and cultures. A public position that aims for broad public support cannot, and should not, fly in the face of the complex and varied beliefs and opinions of the American people.

The right-to-life advocates are attempting, in this diverse society, to enforce their own views. They are ignoring the fact that most Americans continue to support the legalization of abortion and believe the decision should be a matter of personal conscience. The pro-choice advocates have also failed to be sensitive to the varied and often inconsistent beliefs of the American people, even of those who favor their cause. For example, two-fifths of those supporting legalized abortion feel that abortion is morally wrong. Furthermore, women are more likely than men to take this position (Scott, 1989). Failure by pro-choice advocates to consider any compromise, to take account of and even respect the widespread negative feelings about abortion among their supporters and a large number of Americans can, in the long run, alienate those who believe, with some ambivalence, in the right of a woman to make a choice.

Finally, the single-minded arguments about rights have tended to stand alone rather than to be understood in the context of the social and economic conditions that have an impact on the lives of people and the choices they are able to make.

The legal right to have an abortion is not an isolated issue but should be a fail-safe protection and only one part of an integrated and available group of services that pertain to the conception, birth, and rearing of children—what might be called procreative freedom. Such services would include extensive reproductive health education available to all, free and universally available contraception information and devices, and the investment of public funds in research to discover improved contraceptive methods for men as well as women. It is interesting to note that in the midst of the clamor against abortion, public funding for family planning has declined (Forrest & Singh, 1990).

Universally available prenatal care should also be included, along with universal health insurance that includes maternity benefits, family care, maternity and paternity leave with job security guarantees, flextime, job sharing and other workplace adjustments to support parenthood, neighborhood and workplace-based day care, and income support that will keep those who wish to have and rear children out of poverty. It is only in the context of such services and supports that all Americans can truly choose to parent or not to parent.

Privacy is a valued right, and people must be allowed to make crucial personal decisions without state intrusion. But the right to privacy must not be interpreted as the right to be left alone, as the right, finally, to be abandoned.

References

Copelon, R. (1990). From privacy to autonomy: The conditions of sexual and reproductive freedom. In M. G. Fried (Ed.), *From abortion to reproductive freedom* (pp. 27–44). Boston: South End Press.

Davis, A. (1990). Racism, birth control, and reproductive rights. In M. G. Fried (Ed.), *From abortion to reproductive freedom* (pp. 15–26). Boston: South End Press.

Forrest, J. D., & Singh, S. (1990). Public sector savings resulting from expenditures for contraceptive services. *Family Planning Perspective, 22,* 6–15.

Glendon, M. A. (1991). *Rights talk: The impoverishment of political discourse.* New York: Free Press.

Ketchum, S. A. (1984). The bodies of persons. *Social Theory and Social Practice, 10,* 25–38.

Pfeiffer, R. (1985). Abortion policy and the argument from uncertainty. *Social Theory and Practice 11,* 371–386.

Scott, J. (1989). Conflicting beliefs about abortion: Legal approval and moral doubts. *Social Psychology Quarterly, 52,* 319–326.

Willis, E. (1990). Pulling women back into the abortion debate. In M. G. Fried (Ed.), *From abortion to reproductive freedom* (pp. 131–138). Boston: South End Press.

First published November 1991

Health Care: Privilege or Entitlement?

Our health care system is in trouble. Americans are aware of this and are demanding major change. We are spending an enormous amount of our nation's resources on health care—12 percent of our gross national product, which is 50 percent more than the average of all other industrialized countries. In 1990, we spent more than $2,000 per person, compared with $1,000 among our industrialized competitors. The rise in health care costs has been twice the rate of inflation over the past decade (National Association of Social Workers [NASW], 1991).

In spite of this considerable investment of resources and our highly skilled and well-equipped medical system, by most measures the overall health status of Americans lags behind that of many other nations. Among the nations of the world, the United States ranks 12th in life expectancy, 19th in infant morality, 21st in deaths of children under five, and 29th in the percentage of low-birthweight babies. Our low immunization rates are a national disgrace. In 1989, more than 15,000 cases of measles were reported, 10 times more than were reported in 1983, and polio, a disease we had conquered, is reappearing (Children's Defense Fund, 1990). What is wrong?

First, and perhaps most fundamental, is the fact that our health care system is trapped in

> our inability to discuss and decide, as a nation, whether basic health care is a social good that is intrinsically related to individual liberty, independence, and equal opportunity and, therefore, a collective obligation or a

private good to be left as an individual responsibility.
(Shapiro, 1991, p. 6)

We believe that people have a right to life, at least when no exot-
ic intervention is required to maintain it, but we are not clear
about whether they have a right to health. This ambivalence
plays out every day in our hospital emergency rooms. Hospitals
have an obligation, both legal and moral, to snatch people from
the jaws of death and thus must respond when medically indigent
people in desperate condition arrive at their doors. Because preventive, secondary, or early tertiary care is not available to many
of these people, they do not obtain intervention until their conditions have seriously deteriorated and their care is much more
costly.

Second, our health care system has been very much
affected by the changing position of national leadership concerning the collective obligation to provide care. Until Ronald
Reagan's presidency the federal government had moved steadily
toward assuming more responsibility for the health of the nation,
particularly for the most vulnerable populations. Medicare,
Medicaid, and maternal and child health programs developed and
flourished. Hopes were high for a national health plan, and such
plans were brought to the Congress for action by Presidents
Nixon and Carter, only to be casualties of the cross fire between
liberals and conservatives in the Congress.

However, in the past decade this trend has been reversed.
The past decade has seen a steady reduction in the federal government's involvement and expenditures in health care. Programs
have been widely and deeply cut, and the responsibility for the
financing of care has been steadily shifted to the patient, the family, and localities. Cost-containment measures, such as diagnosis-
related groups, have limited hospital stays and shifted the burden
of care to families at the same time that the programs that might
support families in providing care have been reduced or eliminat-
ed. A case in point has been the veto of the Family Leave Act,
which at no cost to the government supports the family caring
for an ill member at home. Expenses also have been curtailed
through reductions in the number of people covered by federal
health insurance programs. For example, eligibility requirements

for Medicaid have been increased to the point that only 42 percent of those who are below the poverty line are covered (White, 1991).

Our national health care policy also has supported the drift toward privatization and toward an increasingly market-driven health care system. This Social Darwinian view of the distribution of health care services leads dramatically to the survival, not necessarily of the fittest, but of those with the greatest power and command of resources and those with the most extensive and generous insurance coverage.

The combination of privatization and competition has led to the development of for-profit medical facilities that can cream off well-insured high-fee-paying patients, leaving the voluntary hospitals and particularly the public city and county hospitals to care for those without resources and often those who are the sickest. This competition and neglect have promoted a two- or three-track health care system based on ability to pay.

Furthermore, the distribution and character of health care have been altered by the enormously influential presence of third-party payers. Although cost-containment efforts have led to shorter hospital stays and sharply limited mental health and other services, the reimbursement system also rewards more intensive and extensive intervention. Laboratory and medical tests can be extremely profitable for the provider and therefore may be ordered more frequently than absolutely necessary. It is much easier to charge the distant and impersonal company than the individual in the office, but in the long run, we all pay. Ornish (1990) wrote, in his volume on heart disease,

> The third party reimbursement system encourages the use of drugs and surgery rather than health education. In America, more money is spent on treating heart disease than any other illness—$87 billion annually. . . . If I perform bypass surgery on a patient, the insurance company will pay at least $30,000. If I perform a balloon angioplasty on a patient, the insurance company will pay at least $7,500. If I spend the same amount of time teaching a heart patient about nutrition and stress management techniques, the insurance company will

pay no more than $150. If I spend that time teaching a
well person how to stay healthy, the insurance company will not pay at all. (p. 28)

The state of our health care system is of vital concern to
all social workers, personally and professionally. Not only do tens
of thousands of social workers work in health and mental health,
but the welfare of every client in any setting is intimately tied to
his or her health and the health of family members. The distribution of health care is a matter of social well-being and of social
justice and therefore is of crucial interest to all social workers and
to the profession. To begin to reform the health care system,
three major and interrelated issues must be resolved: access, cost,
and the nature and definition of health care, which has been primarily defined as sickness care.

Because Americans have not considered health care a
universal entitlement or right and have largely left it to the individual to achieve, millions of Americans are without access.
Thirty-seven million Americans have no public or private health
insurance, a 38 percent increase since 1977 (NASW, 1991). Many
more are underinsured. Private insurance companies are increasing exclusions, deductibles, and copayments, shifting more of the
cost burden to the consumer. Courts have been upholding
employers' rights to limit coverage in cases of serious illness
("Employers Winning," 1992). In most states, insurers have the
right to test and refuse anyone who tests positive for the human
immunodeficiency virus, and some have even tried to refuse coverage to people on the basis of occupation or zip code ("Access
to Health Care," 1991).

To even begin to make sure that all Americans have
access to basic health care, we must take the position that basic
health care is a right and that costs should be shared. This fundamental assumption must then be operationalized through a
national health plan that ensures access for all. NASW has developed and is promoting a plan that proposes a federally administered single-payer system (White, 1991). In this issue [May 1992],
Alvin L. Schorr [pp. 263–265] reviews and analyzes different programs and maintains that only a single-payer system can deal with
the current inequities. We must act on access to health care. The

human costs and the costs to our nation and our future of uncared-for people, children without immunization, undiagnosed and untreated illnesses, and people suffering mental and emotional pain without care cannot be tolerated any further.

The cost of health care is sapping our national resources, even though many Americans are unserved or underserved. As access is expanded, what about the parallel expansion of cost? As we make basic health care more available to all, we must realize that everyone cannot get everything. This raises the controversial issue of the rationing of health care. Many vociferously oppose rationing on moral and ethical grounds, but we are rationing health care now on the basis of the ability to pay. In the March 1992 issue of *Social Work*, Ed Silverman explored the bioethical issues of neonatal care. His discussion centered around the enormous costs to families and to society of the extraordinary interventions made to keep severely disabled infants alive. Somehow we must face the fact that heroic efforts to forestall death in extreme situations "reduces the resources available for other forms of life-saving and life-enhancing measures" (Silverman, 1992, p. 151). We cannot do it all.

This, of course, leads to the question of how such decisions are to be made. If we do not look the other way and let economic factors ration health care, how will we set priorities? Who will establish the guidelines? Some states have made some priority decisions in the expenditure of public money for health care. For example, Arizona and Oregon had been funding bone marrow, pancreas, heart, and liver transplants but have now reallocated the funds to the support of prenatal care for low-income mothers. This decision, of course, rations care on the basis of ability to pay such that those who are well insured may be provided with extraordinary life-saving interventions and those who must rely on public funds may not. The states, in making this decision, are taking the position that all people are entitled to some care, in this case prenatal, but not to all care. Priorities are built into the decision.

An adequate national health plan clearly must include a means for establishing priorities. It is hoped that these priorities would be operationalized and individualized by teams such as those described by Silverman (1992). The resolution of access and priorities issues will inevitably alter the nature and definition of health care in the United States. Priorities must focus on prevention, health maintenance, and basic care.

In this election year, there is a national call for change in health care delivery. We must seize this opportunity to demand that health care reform be placed high on political agendas. We must study and evaluate the various proposals, insist that candidates take a public stand on health care, and let all office seekers know that we care.

References

Access to health care: A Lambda priority. (1991). *Lambda Update, 8*(2), 1.

Children's Defense Fund. (1990). *S.O.S. America: A children's defense budget.* Washington, DC: Author.

Employers winning right to cut back medical insurance. (1992, March 29). *New York Times*, p. 1.

National Association of Social Workers. (1991). *NASW health care fact sheet.* Silver Spring, MD: Author.

Ornish, D. (1990). *Dr. Dean Ornish's program for reversing heart disease.* New York: Ballantine Books.

Shapiro, H. (1991). *Summer 1991, essay #1.* Unpublished manuscript.

Silverman, E. (1992). Hospital bioethics: A beginning knowledge base for the neonatal social worker. *Social Work, 37*, 150–154.

White, B. (1991, October 24). *Statement in support of health care reform through a single-payer national health care program.* Silver Spring, MD: National Association of Social Workers.

First published May 1992

Families and Children

Children in a Careless Society

⚜

On a recent edition of the evening national news, the beginning of the International Children's Summit was reported. The summit, at which 70 heads of state gathered—more than had ever gathered for any meeting before—was organized as an expression of world concern for the welfare of children. Such reports are usually followed by brief clips on children starving in Ethiopia or Bangladesh. This time, however, the scene shifted to just a few blocks from the shining glass tower of the United Nations in New York City, and the viewers were treated to a lengthy and chilling sequence on what is happening to children in this, the wealthiest nation in the world. There were shots of babies with acquired immune deficiency syndrome and babies damaged by crack who were warehoused in understaffed hospitals and institutions. There was an interview with one homeless young mother who said, her voice choked with tears and rage, "All I want for my daughter is to be able to come after school through the same door she went out in the morning" (NBC Nightly News, September 28, 1990). There were shots of shelters and children living on the streets. The final scenes were of workmen burying dead babies, identified only by numbers, in small pine boxes in a congregate grave. Where were the mourners?

We should all be mourners. We can only hope that the millions of Americans who watch the nightly news might mourn a little and, even more important, turn that mourning into action. However, this does not seem to be happening. The plight of poor people, along with the plight of millions of children, in this country is so desperate and overwhelming that the American public may be using psychic numbing to protect itself from the pain and terror, in the same way that we have defended against knowing and believing in the possibility of a nuclear holocaust.

What is happening in this country? How is it that this society, which is supposed to be so child-centered, can be guilty of such unconscionable neglect? The most obvious thing that has happened in the past decade has been the upward shift of wealth and of resources on the economic ladder. The United States now leads all major industrialized countries in the gap dividing the rich and the poor (Phillips, 1990). According to Sen. Daniel Patrick Moynihan, "We've become the first society in history in which the poorest group in the population is children" (as cited in Phillips, 1990).

The worsening condition of people who are poor has not been an accident. It has been the outcome of the past decade's federal policy. Ronald Reagan's economic position contained two major thrusts. The first was to increase the capital available to the wealthiest people in the country to encourage investment and entrepreneurship. A major way to accomplish this was through changed tax policies, a reduction in capital gains, and a drop in the top personal income tax bracket from 70 percent to 28 percent, benefiting primarily the top 5 percent of the population (Phillips, 1990).

The second major effort of Reaganomics was to reduce government spending through the curtailment of social programs and to minimize the federal government's role in health, economic security, and education. Cuts in all human services programs, well known to social workers, reduced the resources available to those in need. The effects of these policies have been dramatic. For example, the average income of the 10 percent of families at the bottom of the economic ladder in 1988 was $3,504, down 14.8 percent from 1977, while the average income of the top 10 percent was $166,000, up 16.5 percent for the same period. Particularly shocking is the fact that the incomes of the top 1 percent increased 49.8 percent to $404,566 (Phillips, 1990). At the same time, cuts in Aid to Families with Dependent Children (AFDC) programs narrowed eligibility, and burdensome verification requirements excluded more and more needy families from receiving public assistance. Many working poor people who had received supplemental assistance were excluded or had their assistance greatly reduced. For example, as a result of the Omnibus Budget Reconciliation Act of 1981, which was the first of many assaults on social programs, the average income of working AFDC families declined from 101 percent to 81 percent of the poverty line (Aponte, 1987).

What have been the outcomes for children who suffer a loss of income; a decrease of relief in kind (such as school lunches and food stamps); and a sharp reduction of social, educational, and health care services and housing subsidies?

First, in almost every indicator of child well-being, our record is shocking. Currently, America ranks 19th in infant mortality rate. Black children born in inner-city Boston, a world medical center, have less of a chance of reaching their first birthday than do children born in Panama or Uruguay (Children's Defense Fund, 1990b). Malnutrition, low immunization rates, low birthweight, and lack of prenatal and postnatal care all attest to the neglect of our children's health. But then, we are one of only two industrialized nations that fail to provide children and families with basic health insurance. (The other is South Africa.) A growing number of children are homeless, with estimates as high as 100,000 (Children's Defense Fund, 1990a).

Classrooms are overcrowded, and teachers are overburdened. In the United States, the ratio of school-age children to teachers is 23 to 1. In this category we rank 19th in the world. (Canada's ratio is 13 to 1.) Of the 500,000 children who drop out of school each year, 75 percent are poor. Federal funds for Head Start are available to only one of every six eligible children (Children's Defense Fund, 1990b). Because of the increased hopelessness, helplessness, and alienation that accompany poverty, social dysfunction indicators such as family violence, family dissolution, child abuse and neglect, teenage pregnancy and drug and alcohol abuse are on the rise (Children's Defense Fund, 1990b; Hudson, 1987; Pelton, 1978, 1989). Why are we letting this happen?

There are some strange and conflicting views about children and about families that seem to run deep in the American consciousness. First is the notion that children belong to their parents, or, in Old English terms, are the chattels of their parents.

A second view very much related to the first one, is that the boundaries around a nuclear family are to be inviolate under almost any circumstances. These principles combine to create a society that is very reluctant to interfere with the family, that is deeply individualistic, and that expects parents to take total responsibility for and full care of their children. This reluctance to interfere is expressed in and rationalized by neglect. Somehow, Americans believe that a person's destiny is appropriately determined by the "accident of birth"—by the parents he or she is born to. There is no conviction that children belong to themselves, to the community, or to the future. Thus, if they have been unlucky in terms of their birth, no real effort is made to make available to them and to their families the compensatory supports and services that would give them the equal chance for a better life. Our reluctance to interfere means that we neglect a family until a child is in serious danger (such as abuse or neglect) and then we move in, dismember the family, and take complete control (Pelton, 1989).

Another belief that has grown out of the English Common Law tradition is that children do not have rights as individuals or as citizens. On November 20, 1989, the U.N. General Assembly unanimously approved an international convention on the social, cultural, civil, and political rights of children. One hundred forty-nine countries have signed to participate in or have ratified the convention. The main holdouts are Iran, Iraq, Libya, and the United States. Should a country be known by the company it keeps? What is our excuse? There is opposition to the convention because it prohibits the death penalty for children and does not take an anti-abortion position. No matter how many pious statements are made about children, education, or a thousand points of light, the evidence is all around us. This society is not taking care of its children. Our throw-away culture, seemingly so invested in saving fetuses, is throwing away children. In doing so, we are throwing away our future.

Where is our profession in the middle of this crisis? Social workers are working with and on behalf of families and children in almost every field of practice, as can be seen in the array of articles published in this journal. We have a very special role in the child welfare system. Our profession was born in that system, and the social institution known as child welfare has been primarily a social work domain since the early 1900s.

That system is now in crisis. Overwhelmed by the investigative demands of escalating reports of abuse and neglect, protective services and emergency intervention are driving child welfare (Kammerman & Kahn, 1990). Overburdened staffs must place children to protect them because preventive and in-home services are not available. Social workers are living with the fear and anxiety of leaving children in unsafe situations without services or supervision. The hope for a family-focused preventive and rehabilitative system that was stimulated by the passage of the Child Welfare Reform and Adoption Assistance Act of 1980 (P.L. 96-272) has turned to despair as adequate funds to support the goals of the act have not been forthcoming. Interestingly enough, without federal support, the spirit of the law has found expression in the family preservation movement. The innovative programs and creative social workers that are part of this initiative are demonstrating that most families can function and most at-risk children can remain at home if intensive services are provided. These pilot projects are, perhaps, charting the direction for practice with families and children in the 1990s.

Innovative service programs and imaginative and dedicated social workers who extend themselves far beyond the constraints of struggling agencies and limited programs can save a family or help a child. However, this does not begin to address the terrible circumstances of millions of American children. We must work together to change the priorities of this nation. We must bear witness. We must advocate. We must campaign against those legislators who are cutting social programs and who are refusing to raise the tax rate of people in the highest income bracket. Every 30 years, this country has gone through a period of caring, a period of social reform: the first decade of this century, the 1930s, the 1960s. We are now in the 1990s. Let's all make it happen.

References

Aponte, R. (1987). Urban poverty: A state-of-the-art review of the literature. In W. J. Hudson (Ed.), *The truly disadvan-*

taged. *The inner city, the underclass, and public policy* (pp. 165–187). Chicago: University of Chicago Press.

Children's Defense Fund. (1990a). *Children 1990. A report card, briefing book, and action primer.* Washington, DC: Author.

Children's Defense Fund. (1990b). *S.O.S. America: A children's defense budget.* Washington, DC: Author.

Hudson, W. J. (Ed). (1987). *The truly disadvantaged: The inner city, the underclass, and public policy.* Chicago: University of Chicago Press.

Kammerman, S. B., & Kahn, A. J. (1990, Winter). If CPS is driving child welfare—Where do we go from here? *Public Welfare,* pp. 9–13.

Pelton, L. H. (1978). Child abuse and neglect: The myth of classlessness. *American Journal of Orthopsychiatry, 48,* 608–617.

Pelton, L. H. (1989). *For reasons of poverty.* New York: Praeger.

Phillips, K. (1990). *The politics of rich and poor: Wealth and the American electorate in the Reagan aftermath.* New York: Random House.

First published November 1990

Violence and Families
Liane V. Davis

Over the past decade I have watched with concern as social workers have joined the crusade to privatize violence in families. Until the 1970s, the term "domestic violence" described urban riots (Tierney, 1982). Now it describes violence in the home. The change in meaning, perhaps unintentional, has paralleled a change in the social work profession's concern: We examine violence in the home and sometimes forget the violence that families live amid and the violence done to them by social institutions.

I sometimes believe I am out of step with the profession, yearning for my practicum days when social workers understood the connections between social and family pathology and tried to change the conditions under which people lived rather than the people themselves. Elizabeth A. Segal's article in this issue [September 1991, pp. 454–457] gives me hope that I am not alone in my nostalgia. She observes,

> The focus of social work practice has shifted from the causes of poverty to the symptoms. . . . Many of the social problems of today—for example, substance abuse, family disintegration, violence, gangs, severe mental illness, and public health concerns—are related to and certainly exacerbated by growing up poor.

We are getting better at treating all kinds of symptoms, but I fear that many of us, despairing of any real social change in these conservative times, have lulled ourselves into believing we are effectively curing problems.

There are other troublesome signs. Neil Gilbert, a distinguished professor of social welfare at the University of California, Berkeley, received national news coverage for his recent attack on feminists. Labeling sexual assault against women and children "the phantom epidemic," he challenged the validity of research on its pervasiveness. In what he must have intended as biting criticism, he wrote, "Radical feminists who promote advocacy numbers aim not so much to solve the problem of sexual assault as to change social perceptions of its basic nature" (Gilbert, 1991, p. 65). Gilbert misses the point. The only way to solve the problem of violence against oppressed people, whether it occurs in the home, on the streets, or on pre–Civil War plantations, is to change social perceptions of its basic nature.

Sexual and physical abuse of children, wives, and elders are not new phenomena. We do not really know whether there is more or less now than in centuries past. What has changed is how we perceive the problems. Gordon (1988) noted that

> Family violence has been historically and politically constructed. . . . The very definition of what constitutes acceptable domestic violence, and appropriate responses to it, developed and then varied according to political moods and the force of certain political movements. (p. 3)

Battered women's shelters did not spring up because there was an upsurge in abused women; child protective services did not develop because more children were being abused and neglected. Instead, services developed because some people decided to do something different about problems that have been around since the beginning of recorded history. As with many other issues, violence in families will fade out of the public's attention not because it has gone away but because it is eclipsed by more pressing concerns that are more congruent with the current sociopolitical agenda. Such as been the case throughout history.

Without an understanding of that history, we are doomed to repeat it. Without a historical perspective, we remain blind to how we as social workers are affected by the larger forces of society. The following brief history of wife abuse in this country, which draws freely from Gordon (1988) and Pleck (1987), illustrates how history repeats itself.

Social workers know well how our society has responded to child abuse. We have gone from "child savers" to "family preservers." At times we have reached into families to protect the children from their cruel parents; at other times we have advocated for social reform to change the conditions under which families neglect and abuse their children. Most recently, we have moved into homes to preserve families and prevent children from being removed.

The history of concern with abused women is less well known. Violence against women threatened the moral order of Puritan society. Neighbors were encouraged to watch over one another and report any serious family violence to the minister, who would then visit the family, counsel them to mend their errant ways, and pray with them for God's forgiveness. Puritan intolerance of wife abuse is reflected by the Massachusetts colony's 1641 Body of Liberties, which assured that "Everie married woman shall be free from bodilie correction or stripes by her husband, unlesse it be in his own defence upon her assault" (Pleck, 1987, p. 22).

Yet there was wide disparity between word and deed. The laws were rarely enforced; between 1633 and 1802, only 23 cases of wife beating, husband beating, assault between master and servant, or incest were heard in the Plymouth courts. Few options were available to abused women. Divorce was unavailable to most; remarriage after divorce was prohibited. The mixed message has been clear since the beginning of this country: Women should not be abused by their husbands, but the state will neither make it easy for women to leave abusing husbands and survive if they do so nor will it punish abusive men.

Morality and family violence issues were joined again during the 19th century. Reframing the issue of battering as an evil of alcohol, the temperance movement got a sympathetic hearing for the "drunkard's wife," whom they painted as an innocent victim of a brutish man. The movement balked, however, at embracing what some believed essential for women to escape from male brutality: securing women's rights. As they left the temperance movement to become outspoken advocates for women, first-wave feminists like Elizabeth Cady Stanton and Susan B. Anthony understood that abuse against women in marriage would stop only when women had the right to divorce, the right to custody of their children, the right to their own earnings, and an equal voice in politics. Stanton spoke out against the institution of marriage itself, seeing it as the source of women's oppression and victimization.

Such a direct challenge to traditional family values was too great a threat in the increasingly conservative era at the end of the century. Even Stanton had to retreat. She continued to advocate liberalizing divorce law but silenced her voice on women's abuse within marriage. By the late 19th century, attention turned to punishing the offenders and holding them responsible for supporting their children. Wife beating became a law-and-order issue.

During the early decades of the 20th century, social workers joined the ranks of the newly developed family court system, a system whose official policy was that of "home mending":

> Reformers during the Progressive period hoped to shore up the male-headed nuclear family, so that children would not have to be removed from abusive and neglectful parents and marriages would not be broken up. (Pleck, 1987, p. 18)

Caseworkers took on the task of reconciling families, sometimes out of their belief that intact, male-headed families were in the best interest of all, sometimes out of their belief that women could not survive economically as single mothers. Divorce was still difficult to obtain; child support, minimal at best, was not always paid.

As the depression years approached, therapeutic models gained ascendance. First came marital treatment, introduced to deal with the domestic discord that sometimes resulted in wife abuse. Therapists were encouraged to take a neutral stance, communicating to husband and wife their shared responsibility. Then came Freudian theory, which led to attempts to fix the masochistic psyches of battered women rather than their marital relationships. Freudian theory legitimated skepticism about the truthfulness of women's and children's reports of their abuse. By the late 1930s, the American Bar Association was advising judges to order sexual assault victims to undergo psychiatric examinations because it was a well-known psychiatric "fact" that they frequently confused fantasy and reality. Psychiatrists and psychiatric social workers were trained to avoid asking patients about their childhood experience with violence and to doubt the truthfulness of their accounts.

More than vestiges of this history remain with us, as several articles in this issue reveal. The truthfulness of children's accounts of violence, broadly challenged today, is discussed by Gwat-Yong Lie and Anjanette Inman [pp. 396–399] and by Mary Ann Mason [pp. 391–395]. Stephen M. Rose, Carolyn G. Peabody, and Barbara Stratigeas [pp. 408–413] demonstrate that mental health professionals still do not ask some people (those with chronic mental illness) about their experiences with childhood abuse.

The history of violence in families is a history of changing social perceptions about what is wrong and right and about what is harmful and not harmful. Gordon (1988) observed that "the very definition of family violence is by no means established. Ultimately we may all have to define for ourselves, for our own lives the border between acceptable and unacceptable attempts to coerce" (p. 291).

The history of violence in families is a history of changing language. Mimi Abramovitz states in this issue [pp. 380–384] that "Benign sounding terms . . . contain buried metaphors about women, race, and poverty . . . that, in some cases, violate the interests of those they seek to describe." Calling rape "sexual assault" and wife battering "domestic violence" changes reality. It is men who rape women; it is husbands who batter wives. These acts occur within a social context of male power and female oppression.

Battering, rape, and sexual abuse occur within a larger environment that bombards us with conflicting messages about violence. Consider the front page of my local newspaper one day early this summer: The large headline at the top of the page read, "A Boy's Dream Blossoms as Exploits in the Desert." I read the story with more than passing interest because I knew the "boy's" mother was a social work student. The story told of a returning war hero's remarkable feat: He had destroyed 23 Iraqi tanks and crippled 10 others all in a normal 12-hour war day. He described his exploit: "When the war was over, I didn't want to look back on a mission and see that I passed up an opportunity to blow something up. . . . It was just a lot of fun. There's no way to describe seeing the tanks burn" (Spivak, 1991, p. 1). As I read the story, I wondered how many people he had killed in the tanks. But there was no body count, no acknowledgment that burning tanks burn people.

The headline at the bottom of the page was in smaller type: "Curfew for Children under 16 Proposed to KC Council." The statistics were alarming: In 1990, 20 juveniles were arrested for murder or manslaughter, 35 for rape, and 145 for aggravated assault.

How can we expect our children to understand that it is morally reprehensible to hurt others, when we welcome the Gulf War heroes home with multimillion dollar parades and ignore the fact that they killed 100,000 people? How can we expect women to lovingly care for their children when they are forced to bear unwanted children and then deprived of the resources to care adequately for themselves and their families? How can we expect women to leave abusive men when they know they may become another homeless statistic?

Why do we as a profession struggle so hard to keep the environment in focus? Why do we fall back on blaming the victim, even when we do not intend to? Why have we responded to violence in families with treatment models to teach people to communicate better with one another? Why have we adopted the conservative metaphor of family preservation as our slogan? Abramovitz also points out that

> although social workers know that conservative ideas
> have captured the social welfare policy agenda, few
> appreciate the extent to which their personal and pro-
> fessional language contains unspoken messages that
> may not be their own.

I hope the unspoken messages are not our own, but I worry that we have bought into them all too well. Terms such as "dysfunctional family" come as readily to our students (and faculty and practitioners) as they do to Geraldo and Oprah. Students enter schools of social work with well-formed ideas about the dysfunction in their own families and sincere commitments to learn the clinical skills to enable them to eradicate dysfunction in other families. In school and in their field agencies, many find the clinical models they eagerly apply.

But clinical models are not enough. Families are microcosms of society. Those made powerless by our social institutions are oppressed within their homes. We need to develop our skills as social practitioners, becoming as committed and effective at changing oppressive social conditions as we are at changing oppressive family conditions.

References

Gilbert, N. (1991, Spring). Sexual assault: The phantom epidemic. *Public Interest*, pp. 54–65.

Goldstein, D., & Krekeler, C. (1991, June 1). Curfew for children under 16 proposed to KC council. *Kansas City Star*, p. 1.

Gordon, L. (1988). *Heroes of their own lives: The politics and history of family violence.* New York: Penguin.

Pleck, E. (1987). *Domestic tyranny. The making of American social policy against family violence from colonial times to the present.* New York: Oxford University Press.

Spivak, J. (1991, June 1). A boy's dream blossoms as exploits in the desert. *Kansas City Star*, p. 1.

Tierney, K. J. (1982). The battered women movement and the creation of the wife-beating problem. *Social Problems, 29*, 207–220.

Liane V. Davis, MSW, PhD, is associate professor and associate dean, University of Kansas School of Social Welfare. Her scholarship addresses areas of concern to women: woman abuse, reproductive rights, and sexual harassment. She has applied feminist thought to social work practice and research. Currently she is developing and evaluating a strengths-based model for delivering case management services to the primarily women clients in Kansas's version of the Job Opportunities and Basic Skills Training Program.

First published September 1991

Family Ties

W henever discussion turns to the state of the American family, a consensus quickly emerges. The family is under severe stress and we must be concerned about its welfare, even its survival. Certainly the welfare of the family has long been a major focus of the social work profession. Our first professional journal was called *The Family*. Casework was born and developed in the Charity Organization Societies, later renamed Family Service Societies. Mary Richmond (1917), a founder of the profession, defined the *family* as the unit of service or the unit of attention and warned that good results of "individual treatment would crumble away" if social workers failed to take account of the family (p. 134).

"The family itself," she was convinced, "continued to be the pivotal institution around which our human destinies revolve" (Richmond, 1930, p. 262). Building on this strong and rich tradition, and expressing widely held concerns, the National Association of Social Workers (NASW) this spring [1990] inaugurated a two-year public service campaign focused on strengthening the American family, adopting the phrase "Family Ties" as its motto. I am sure that most social workers will applaud this decision and embrace this theme. After all, who could be against strengthening the American family?

However, if we take this theme seriously, not just as public relations rhetoric but as a professional mission, what does it really mean for the way we think and work? How does it shape our practice, our view of the world, our definition of problems and solutions?

Perhaps the first question to ask as we stop to explore the meaning of our theme is, What is the American family like? How may it be defined? There is no specific or generally agreed-on answer to this question. In fact, it was over this very issue, the definition of the family, that Jimmy Carter's White House Conference on the Family foundered in the late 1970s. Certainly the shape, the very structure of the family, is changing, and there is more variety in family forms. The ideal American family of the 1950s of "Father Knows Best" fame, if it ever came close to representing reality, now lives primarily in memory and fantasy. The family that consists of a first-time married couple with two or three children, the father working and the mother at home, has almost ceased to exist.

What has happened to this family? Perhaps the most far-reaching and revolutionary change has been the wholesale movement of American wives and mothers into the work force. Today, 60 percent of mothers of children younger than 18 work outside the home, and it is expected that in five years that figure will have grown to 80 percent. The divorce rate has dramatically altered the structure of the family. Today 50 percent of all first marriages will end in divorce. Seventy-five percent of these divorced people remarry, and 60 percent of them will divorce again. More than one-third of all children born since 1980 will live with a stepparent.

Families are smaller in that fewer children are being born in nuclear families, but families are getting larger and more complex as they become extended through remarriage. As a result of divorce, the number of single-parent households, most of which are headed by women, is growing. In 1955, 10 percent of American families were headed by single-parents. Today the figure is at least 25 percent and increasing. Included in these figures are the many teenagers who become mothers, two-thirds of whom are unmarried and 94 percent of whom keep their babies.

Adding to the diversity of the American family are childless couples, unmarried partners of all ages living together, and lesbian and gay couples with or without children. If we are to strengthen the American family, does this not include the ties in all these kinds of intimate groups? How then is the family to be defined? The U.S. Bureau of the Census's definition is well known and sharply limiting: "Two or more persons related by birth, marriage, or adoption who reside in the same household" ("Twenty-first Century Family," 1989–1990, p. 18). A narrow definition of the family recently was challenged successfully in the New York Supreme Court, which set four standards for a family: (1) The exclusivity and longevity of a relationship, (2) the level of emotional and financial commitment, (3) how the people conducted their daily lives and held themselves out to society, and (4) the reliance placed on one another for daily services ("Twenty-first Century Family," 1989–1990).

In announcing the "Family Ties" public service campaign, NASW chose a broad and inclusive view, defining the family in terms of self-definition and function as "two or more individuals who consider themselves family and who assume typical family obligations." But if we are to assume this inclusive definition of the family, if we are going to support and protect family ties in all their shapes and forms, what does it mean for practice?

We must first recognize that the proliferation of family forms does not necessarily mean that the American family is headed for extinction. Rather, it is possible that such changes are a measure of human adaptability and flexibility in a rapidly changing world. We must divest ourselves of the lingering image of the 1950s family as the norm and cease to define all other families that do not fit this image as deficient. This normative–deficit perspective is in our language, in our procedures, and in our policies. We still refer to "broken homes," and our agency fact sheets generally communicate an expectation for a particular family form: "husband, wife, children, and others in household."

Instead we must come to know different kinds of families and learn about their special characteristics, their strengths, and their vulnerabilities. For example, even the idealized family of the 1950s, once nostalgia is set aside, had both strengths and vulnerabilities. The alienation of the distant father working long hours away from the family was described by Osherson (1986) in *Finding Our Fathers* as nothing less than a tragedy. Luepnitz (1988) examined the traditional family as a historical–political construction that is "patriarchal and father absent" and that devalues and blames women. Women, often isolated and overburdened with the almost total care of the children and housework, were highly vulnerable to depression.

We hear about the vulnerabilities of female-headed, single-parent families. Certainly they are economically vulnerable because child care is unavailable and expensive, and employed women face low pay and discrimination. We have been less ready to try to learn about some of the potential strengths of this particular structure. Marianne Walters (personal communication), for example, discovered that because children in such families often carry meaningful responsibilities and contribute genuinely needed services to the family, they often develop important skills, competence, and self-esteem. She thus reframed the pathologized view of the "parentified child." Were we to look, we might find other special characteristics and strengths that emerge in a family when a woman establishes the values, the rituals, and the ways of being together. If we abandon our deficit perspective and stop using the traditional nuclear family as a norm, we may begin to ask the questions and listen to the answers that will tell us what different kinds of families really are like.

Therefore, to shape our practice to support the American family, we must come to a definition of the family that includes all families and develop procedures, policies, and practices that identify and validate these varied and powerful but fragile intimate relationship systems that we call "the family."

Next, we must shape our policies, programs, and practice to support family ties and strengthen and empower the family. Perhaps each of us, whether we are developing and administering policies or programs or delivering direct services to clients, can ask ourselves the following questions. These questions provide a yardstick to measure the extent to which our practice is sensitive and responsive to the family.

• Is our practice based on an understanding that people are part of current and intergenerational family systems and that these human connections are powerful, persistent, and essential to the welfare of the individual?

• Does our practice include, support, and strengthen these important human connections?

• Does our practice involve the family to the fullest extent possible in defining problems and creating solutions, or does it replace a family function in a situation where, with help, the family itself could meet the needs of its members?

• Does our practice move toward separation, hospitalization, or institutionalization only as a last resort? And when separation is required, do we facilitate ongoing family connections?

• Is our practice sensitive to the diversity of family life, flexible in adapting to the different needs of families of different cultures, lifestyles, structures, or life stage?

• In partnership with families, does our practice empower and enhance the family's autonomy, cohesion, competence, and self-esteem?

Finally, having defined the family and suggested criteria for a family perspective, we must consider the problems and issues American families, and all who would work to help strengthen and preserve families, face today. NASW's "Family Ties" campaign identified nine areas important to the strength of America's families: education, health, mental health, child protection, caregiving, economic security, peace, social justice, and global development.

In the pages of this journal [May 1990], we meet social workers who are focused on the welfare of families and children and struggling to learn more, to understand, to surface problems, to find solutions. We are exposed to the breadth of the profession's concerns but also to the extent to which these concerns are family concerns. We learn about women at work, the stresses they face, and their coping strategies. We learn more about the caregiving crisis, about the growing burden placed on families in caring for the frail elderly, the deinstitutionalized mentally ill, and those with chronic physical illness. We learn about the failures of the educational system to meet the needs of minority children and young people. And we learn about the failure of the mental health system, historically and in the present day, in providing services to families of mentally ill children. We learn about family breakdown, about the need for permanency planning for children so that they may be either with their birth family or permanently with a substitute family. And we learn about the high human costs of the abuse of children. But perhaps the most important and the most painful lesson is to be found in the Op-

Ed contribution, "A Social Worker's Agony: Working with Children Affected by Crack/Cocaine" [pp. 197–199], which describes what can happen in families that are destroyed and what can happen to the social worker who deals with them.

References

Luepnitz, D. (1988). *The family interpreted: Feminist theory in clinical practice*. New York: Basic Books.

Osherson, S. (1986). *Finding our fathers. The unfinished business of manhood*. New York: Free Press.

Richmond, M. (1917). *Social diagnosis*. New York: Russell Sage.

Richmond, M. (1930). *The long review*. New York: Russell Sage.

Twenty-first Century Family. (Winter 1989–Spring 1990). *Newsweek, 114* (Special issue).

First published May 1990

Murphy Brown, Dan Quayle, and the American Family

In May 1992, Vice President Dan Quayle, addressing a San Francisco audience, commented on "family values": "It doesn't help matters when prime-time TV has Murphy Brown, a character who supposedly epitomizes today's intelligent, highly paid, professional woman, mocking the importance of fathers by bearing a child alone, and calling it just another lifestyle choice" (Yang & Devroy, 1992, p. A17). The previous Monday, more than 38 million Americans had watched Murphy Brown, on the season finale of the television show of the same name, give birth to a son in a funny, moving, and very human episode. The response to Quayle's comments may well have been registered on the Richter scale as Americans jumped in to debate the pros and cons of Brown's choice and Quayle's criticism.

Quayle, delighted by the chance to steal headlines and breathe life into a lackluster Republican presidential campaign, continued during the remainder of his three-day tour to attack before the press and other audiences what he identified as the "cultural elite," who believe moral truths are relative, who "seem to think the family is an arbitrary arrangement of people who decide to live under one roof, that fathers are dispensable, and that parents need not be married or even be opposite sexes" (Quindlen, 1992, p. E19).

Thus the topic of family values, hardly a new issue, was placed in the center of the 1992 presidential campaign as each candidate rushed to demonstrate his commitment to and his personal exemplification of the values of the American family. Never have we been treated to such intimate inside views of the joys, conflicts, and tragedies of the candidates' family lives; never have young children and the roles of candidates' wives been so important to the image-building process. We have witnessed the Quayles' disagreement over how they should handle the abortion issue should their 13-year-old daughter become pregnant. We have shared the memory of the Gores' agony when their young son lay between life and death after a near-fatal automobile accident. We have heard about the Bushes' loss of a three-year-old daughter to leukemia and have seen Barbara Bush take a leading role as the ingenuous and ideal American grandmother. We have followed the public exploration of Bill Clinton's alleged extramarital affair and debated whether Hillary Rodham Clinton, a successful attorney, is a properly attentive wife and mother (indeed, whether it is possible to be a good mother and work outside of the home).

As we are deluged with masses of campaign texts and thousands of soundbites, it is important to ask: What is this all about? What are the family values? What is the definition of "family"? Why have these issues captured center stage? To what extent are any families valued? And perhaps most important, why should personal morals and private behavior be the business of government?

What Are "Family Values"?

Sometimes family values seems to mean the values that families ought to hold, what families ought to value. My own vision immediately comes to mind: mutual caring and responsibility; loyalty and fidelity; and respect of members' individuality, independence, and privacy. We all understand these values; we were raised with them, and we attempt to express them in our lives and pass them on to our children. However, each family seems to have a different set of values that grow out of cultural and religious beliefs, lived experience, and an idiosyncratic family heritage. Each of us tends to have the deep conviction that our values are both self-evident and right. Instead of exploring and enhancing an understanding of diversity in our nation, there appears to be an agenda set by Quayle and others to move toward a consensus that would be neither possible nor desirable. Quayle and others who would bring these issues into the public arena would do well to heed the words of the great theologian Reinhold Niebuhr: "Religion is frequently a source of confusion in political life and so frequently dangerous to democracy precisely because it introduces absolutes into the realm of relative values" (quoted by Frohnmayer, 1992, p. E19).

What Is a "Family"?

Murphy Brown has been called a poor role model, but it seems remarkable that her show brought forth such censure when there is silence about the continual diet of violence in the media, remarkable that the Bush administration appointed Arnold Schwartzenegger, star of the ultraviolent *Terminator* movies, to chair the President's Council on Physical Fitness and Sports. Are the values of the Terminator to be preferred? What made Murphy's choice so disturbing? Was it family values or a particular definition of the family that was being challenged?

Quayle's agenda implies that only one form of the family is to be valued or even defined as a family. The definition of family and a woman's role within it are important and have always been debated, most acrimoniously since former President Jimmy Carter's 1970s White House Conference on the Family foundered on these issues. The definition of and roles within a family have become an increasingly important social policy issue as the percentage of American families that fit the 1950s definition of the family has shrunk while social policies have failed to keep pace with change. When policies that support families are directed at groups that fit the "official" definition and all intimate domestic systems that do not meet the criteria are disadvantaged, the question of "equal treatment under the law" is raised.

Currently, in spite of Quayle and others, new definitions of the family are being fashioned in the courts, city councils, employment policies, and state legislatures. Gay and lesbian activists have frequently brought the issue forward, but the resulting broadening of the definition is to the advantage of all families that do not fit into the more narrow definitions. For example, in the ground-breaking case *Braschi v. Stahl Associates*, New York State's highest court found that a longtime partner of a man who had died could retain a lease on the rent-controlled apartment the two men had shared. Because leases are transferable only to cohabiting family members, the court, in making this historic decision, stated that the government's proper definition of "family" should not "rest on fictitious legal distinctions or genetic history, but instead should find its foundation in the reality of family life." The opinion in the case set forth the following criteria for determining family status: (1) the degree of emotional commitment and interdependence, (2) interwoven social life, (3) financial interdependence (sharing household expenses, duties, joint checking or savings accounts, life insurance, wills, and so forth), (4) cohabitation, (5) longevity, and (6) exclusivity. In another decision, a lower court in New York City upheld gay and lesbian partners' rights to spousal insurance and health care benefits. In July 1992, several municipal governments enacted domestic-partner legislation and registration, and some states are considering such legislation.

Other cases, however, have had different outcomes. Perhaps best known is the case of domestic partners Sharon Kowalski and Karen Thompson, which tragically demonstrates the lack of protection afforded alternative families. Karen fought in the Minnesota courts for 10 years for the right to maintain contact with Sharon, who was severely disabled with a brain-stem injury in an automobile accident. Karen also fought to obtain the best medical care for Sharon, for guardianship, and eventually for Sharon's return to the home they had shared, as Sharon wished. However, the courts awarded Sharon's father sole custody. He placed Sharon in an inadequate nursing home where her condition markedly deteriorated, and he refused to allow Karen to see her, although the hours of patient care and social stimulation Karen had provided had figured prominently in Sharon's rehabilitation. Although Sharon's family finally relinquished custody, it may be too late for her to regain all she lost during the years of minimal care (Griscom, 1992). An analysis of the "family values" demonstrated in this situation could be instructive.

Why Have these Issues Captured Center Stage?

The current concern about the definition of the family may be an expression of a backlash in relation to the growing recognition of a wider variety of family forms and the view that "family" is defined primarily by behavior and by personal choice and commitment. This backlash is concretely demonstrated by the placement on the Colorado State ballot of a proposal that would bar any civil rights measures specifically intended to protect homosexuals. This proposal was sponsored by Colorado for Family Values, a group whose battle cry is "stop gay activists before they trample on your freedoms" ("A Vote Could Bar Gay-Rights Laws," 1992, p. 31).

How Much Are Families Valued?

To what extent is there willingness to establish public policies to support the family, to make use of our national resources to improve the quality of the lives of American families? The Reagan and Bush administrations' record of action in relation to family values belies the rhetoric. Tax and welfare policy would indicate that rich families are valued, middle-class families are ignored, and poor families are devalued (Phillips, 1990). The dismantling of social and maternal and child health programs; the lack of action around a national health care plan; and the reduction of Title XX funds, which provide monies to the states for most family support programs, point to a disinterest in the welfare of families. Even when there has been no cost to the government, George Bush has not demonstrated that he values the family. In 1990, he vetoed the Family Leave Act, which would have required employers of more than 50 employees to give limited, unpaid, job-protected leave for childbirth, adoption, or the serious illness of a family member. His recent record is no better. Bush promised in his State of the Union address in January 1992 that he would increase the tax exemption for each dependent child by $500, but his promise has not been kept. Bush has opposed Congress on a bipartisan move to increase expenditures for Head Start. Bills in the House that would increase spending for child welfare, particularly for family preservation programs, have languished.

As the "family values" discussion continues, let us ask which local, state, and national candidates by their actions actually demonstrate that they value families—all kinds of families—by proposing and advocating for actions that really support these crucial, valuable, tough, yet vulnerable human systems.

References

Braschi v. Stahl Associates, State of New York, Court of Appeals, July 6, 1989, Case 108.

Frohnmayer, J. E. (1992, June 14). Is that what he meant? *New York Times*, p. E19.

Griscom, J. L. (1992). The case of Sharon Kowalski and Karen Thompson: Ableism, heterosexism, and sexism. In P. S. Rothenberg (Ed.), *Race, class, and gender in the United States: An integrated study*. New York: St. Martin's Press.

Phillips, K. (1990). *The politics of the rich and the poor*. New York: Random House.

Quindlen, A. (1992, June 14). Digging a divide. *New York Times*, p. E19.

A vote could bar gay-rights laws. (1992, May 24). *New York Times*, p. 31.

Yang, J. E., & Devroy, A. (1992, May 21). Quayle: 'Hollywood doesn't get it'. *Washington Post*, pp. A1, A17.

First published September 1992

Family Preservation
under Attack

In June 1993, Patrick Murphy, the Cook County, Illinois, Public Guardian, whose role it is to represent abused children, mounted a vicious attack on family preservation programs, entitled "Family Preservation and Its Victims," on the op-ed page of the *New York Times*. Published with an ugly illustration that drew readers' attention to the presentation, the article took the position that "in most cases, giving services and money to parents who have abused or neglected their children can do nothing but reward irresponsible and even criminal behavior" (p. 21). Murphy represents a version of the antiquated social control principle of "less eligibility," which states that people in trouble and troubled people should be punished, not helped.

He continued his discussion by telling the tragic stories of two children who died in their own homes—one through abuse and the other through neglect—after the families had participated in a family preservation program. This, he wrote, is how family preservation works in real life. Unfortunately, his views have been welcomed and repeated by others, and we are now witnessing a backlash against one of the most creative, interesting, and potentially effective programmatic and practice approaches developed in child and family services in years.

The attack, of course, was well timed; it appeared just when Congress was considering the Clinton administration's budget and whether to include the Family Preservation and Child Welfare Reform Act in federal spending plans. Similar legislation managed to get through both houses of Congress in 1992 but was vetoed by President George Bush. The fate of the 1993 version hangs in the balance in the current conference negotiations between the House and the Senate. The bill, strongly supported by the National Association of Social Workers, includes provisions that will promote prevention and early intervention services (family preservation), strengthen families, address the needs of children in out-of-home care, and expand adoption assistance at the cost of $1.2 billion over the next five years.

It is the family preservation initiative that has drawn fire. Wrote Murphy, "The family preservation system is a continuation of the sloppy thinking of the 1960s and the 1970s that holds as an unquestionable truth, that society should never blame a victim. Of course the children are never considered victims here. Rather the parents are considered victims of poverty and addiction" (p. 21). On the other hand, family preservation has been widely heralded over the past decade. National and international conferences have been held, volumes have been written, and Bill Moyers's impressive and moving documentary (*Families First*, which aired on PBS on March 25, 1992) presented family preservation to the American television viewer. In the midst of this controversy and passion, it would be useful to step back and consider family preservation, to explore the history of the movement, to define what it is and isn't, and to examine its purpose and potential.

Development of Family Preservation

Although the roots of family preservation go back as far as the St. Paul, Minnesota, Family-Centered Project of the 1950s (Birt, 1956) and probably back to the work of Mary Richmond at the turn of the century, modern family preservation developed as an attempt to realize the goals of the landmark Adoption Assistance and Child Welfare Act of 1980 (P.L. 96-272), which was signed into law with high hopes and enthusiasm. This legislation, developed in response to the growing concerns about children adrift in the foster care system, radically changed public child welfare philosophy and policy. The act took the position that every child has a right to a permanent home if possible, first with his or her biological parents, and if that is impossible, in an adoptive family or in substitute care as similar as possible to the family. This position was a translation into the child welfare system of the widely held principle valuing the "least-restrictive environment," which has guided many federal social policies in recent decades. Specifically, the act defined child welfare services broadly and established the principle that reasonable efforts must be made to prevent the unnecessary separation of children from their families (Samantrai, 1992).

Unfortunately, almost immediately after the bill became law, the Reagan administration came to power, and the process of dismantling the social programs and supports needed to sustain families began. Social agencies and individual workers were put in a double bind; they were expected to keep children at home when the resources needed to do this were disappearing. Furthermore, although the act survived the administration's strategy to fold all programs into block grants, it was never adequately funded. The Family Preservation and Child Welfare Reform Act would begin to devote some resources to the achievement of the goals of P.L. 96-272.

Immediately after the passage of the 1980 act, the numbers of children in out-of-home care began to decline; before long, that trend was reversed. Foster care caseloads grew 65 percent, from 276,000 in 1985 to 429,000 in 1991. Ironically, in spite of the passage of P.L. 96-272, the ratio of foster care expenditures to child welfare service appropriations grew from 2 to 1 in 1981 to 8 to 1 by 1992 (U.S. Government Accounting Office [GAO], 1993). In an effort to stem this tide and to show how the aims of P.L. 96-272 could be achieved despite financial barriers, innovative pilot programs were developed across the country to prevent placement and maintain children in their own homes. Most of these programs, at least in part, modeled themselves on the family preservation model developed by HomeBuilders of Tacoma, Washington, in the mid-1970s (Kinney, Haapala, & Booth, 1991).

The auspices of programs varied. With support from private foundations, agency dollars, and some public funds, many programs started in private agencies and contracted with the public sector. Some adventurous states took the initiative early, despite the barriers that existed to receiving matching federal funds (GAO, 1993). For example, Michigan's Families First program, which was featured on the Bill Moyers show, pioneered by transferring start-up funds from the foster care budget for a pilot family preservation project in 1988. At that time, about 50 private agencies and units of public systems were offering family preservation programs in 15 states. The growth of the family preservation movement in the past five years has been remarkable. Michigan, for example, now has family preservation services available in every one of its 83 counties. By 1993, there were about 400 family preservation programs across the country, and 20 states had made a major commitment to developing services modeled after HomeBuilders.

What Is Family Preservation?

Family preservation is a model of intervention developed very specifically for work with families in which the placement of one or more of the children outside the family is imminent. Drawing on crisis intervention, family systems, life space intervention, ecological, and cognitive-behavioral theories and practices, family preservation is a family-centered, intensive, in-home service available 24 hours a day, seven days a week, for a time-limited period of four to six weeks. Family preservation social workers spend many hours a week with and on behalf of each family and carry a caseload of two or three families at one time. Guided by a "strengths" perspective (Saleebey, 1992), the workers must be flexible and creative generic practitioners who themselves provide or connect families with whatever services and resources are required. Such services include "active aid in the solution of practical problems that contribute to family stress; instruction in parenting skills and in the resolution of family conflicts; on-site monitoring of family members at risk; the development of on-going linkages with formal and informal support systems" (Nelson, 1988, p. 3).

Professionals in child welfare who have long campaigned for the shift of resources to the "front end" of the service continuum were enthusiastic, and reports began to be issued that positively evaluated programs, primarily in terms of sharply reduced placement rates and the amount of money saved over the alternative expenditures for foster care. These reports contributed to the growing enthusiasm. Subsequent research has been more mixed, finding (not surprisingly) that the rates of placement of the children in these families begin to climb as time goes on, raising questions as to the durability of the gains made through family preservation services. Some research has found little significant difference between the outcomes with families in family preservation programs and families in control groups who received standard child welfare services (Wells & Biegel, 1992). These reports have provided ammunition for those who would question the programs and campaign to defeat the current family preservation legislation.

How can we make sense of this confused picture? It seems clear that family preservation is suffering from success. First, as hundreds of programs develop across the country, the standards and characteristics of the programs become more varied, and the original crisis-oriented, immediate-response, family-centered, home-based, intensive, time-limited model begins to be altered. In fact, the term "family preservation" has become so popular that any group doing anything helpful in relation to a family could claim they were doing it. Multiple definitions make the term meaningless. When criticisms are leveled at "family preservation," we are unsure of the characteristics of the program being criticized. Furthermore, the emphasis on saving money, a strategy used to sell the programs to reluctant administrators and legislators, may lead to inadequate, abbreviated, or less-intensive programs that cannot guarantee the first objective of the programs—the safety of the children. Programs that do not contain the key characteristics cannot be expected to function as did the original model that was developed, replicated, and refined over time.

Second, family preservation has been so widely heralded and celebrated that it is in danger of appearing to be the answer to all of the problems posed in protective services, which is a scenario for failure. Family preservation can be only one part of a continuum of child welfare services that should include preventive and supportive work before a situation deteriorates to the crisis stage, as well as longer-term supportive services on an as-needed basis, a range of temporary out-of-home care options as required, family reunification services, and adoption and post-adoption services.

Most troubling is the assumption that family preservation should work when economic, social, community, and health care resources are inadequate or unavailable. In fact, it is troubling that family preservation was born in the context of a politically conservative period. We must not expect that children will be protected and nurtured through the heroic efforts of families and social workers in an uncaring, hostile, and depriving environment. If we focus on family change without attending to the problems in our society, we are, contrary to Murphy's view, blaming the victim. Family preservation can mobilize needed services and resources, but it cannot substitute for such resources. In fact, one study found that "families were more likely to remain intact when services were concrete, such as teaching of family care, supplemental parenting, medical care, help in securing food, and financial services" (Berry, 1992, p. 320).

What Can We Say about Family Preservation?

How can we respond to the criticisms of Murphy and others? What can we say about family preservation?

First, family preservation does what it promises. It operationalizes the principle, enunciated in P.L. 96-272 and often ignored by the courts, that "reasonable efforts" must be made to avoid unnecessary placements of children in out-of-home care. Furthermore, it does preserve families. Reports of programs from the South Bronx to Washington State indicate that from 74 percent to more than 90 percent of the families served in family preservation programs were still intact one year after termination (Barthel, 1992; Cole & Duva, 1990; Kinney et al., 1991; University Associates, 1993).

Second, family preservation does protect children during the period of service. For example, in the first 12 months of Michigan's Families First program, there was only one incident of abuse among the 2,505 children served by the program. Although the abuse of one child is of concern, it must be noted that the National Center on Child Abuse found that 30 children are abused out of every 1,000 in out-of-home care (Barthel, 1992).

A third and not insignificant finding in evaluating family preservation programs is the high morale, enthusiasm, commitment, and conviction on the part of workers, supervisors, and administrators in the programs. For example, in the extensive evaluation of the Families First program, 83 percent of the professionals in the programs were satisfied or very satisfied with their jobs, and 89 percent felt the program was effective or extremely effective. This is in sharp contrast to the burnout, low morale, and powerlessness so common among the staff members of public child welfare agencies. Client families were similarly satisfied with the service, with 98 percent of the families surveyed saying they would recommend Families First to another family in similar circumstances (University Associates, 1993).

Family preservation is not an answer to all our problems. It can neither function without resources nor stand alone without being surrounded by a continuum of child welfare services, but it has proved to be a crucial and effective linchpin in that continuum. Family preservation is a young program, and many research questions must be pursued concerning the value of different characteristics of the model, the value for different families, and the relative effectiveness of the growing number of models of family preservation.

Perhaps one of the most important contributions of family preservation is the window it provides on the lives of the families served. Social workers have long been troubled and discouraged working with some families. In the early years, these families would have been labeled the "undeserving poor"; more recently they have been called "multiproblem," "hard to reach," "severely dysfunctional," and often "untreatable." In the social welfare system, these families have been given just enough resources and help to survive but not enough to prosper. Social workers have never really pursued the question, "How would these families do if they ever really got the help and the resources they needed?" Family preservation is exploring that question on a large scale. We have not been close enough to these families to know them in all their diversity; to know their potential, pain, losses, and wishes; or to go with them through their daily life. It is important that family preservation workers bear witness to the special wisdom these families have gained. It is crucial that they tell us what they have learned from these families. The information could radically change our professional discourse and our practice.

References

Adoption Assistance and Child Welfare Act of 1980, P.L. 96–272, 42 U.S.C. 670.

Barthel, J. (1992). *For children's sake: The promise of family preservation*. New York: Winchell.

Berry, M. (1992). An evaluation of family preservation services: Fitting agency services to family needs. *Social Work, 37,* 314–321.

Birt, C. (1956). The family-centered project of St. Paul. *Social Work, 1,* 41–47.

Cole, E., & Duva, J. (1990). *Family preservation: An orientation for administrators and practitioners*. Washington, DC: Child Welfare League of America.

Kinney, J., Haapala, D., & Booth, C. (1991). *Keeping families together: The HomeBuilders model*. Hawthorne, NY: Aldine de Gruyter.

Murphy, P. (1993, June 19). Family preservation and its victims. *New York Times*, p. 21.

Nelson, D. (1988). *Recognizing and realizing the potential of "family preservation"* [mimeo]. Washington, DC: Center for the Study of Social Policy.

Saleebey, D. (1992). *The strengths perspective in social work practice*. New York: Longman.

Samantrai, K. (1992). To prevent unnecessary separation in children and families: Public Law 96–272—Policy and practice. *Social Work, 37,* 295–303.

University Associates. (1993). *Evaluation of Michigan's Families First program, summary report* [photocopy]. Lansing, MI.

U.S. Government Accounting Office, Human Resources Division. (1993). *Foster care: Services to prevent out-of-home placements are limited by funding barriers*. Washington, DC: U.S. Government Printing Office.

Wells, K., & Biegel, D. (1992). Intensive family preservation services research: Current status and future agenda. *Social Work Research & Abstracts, 25*(1), 21–27.

First published September 1993

The Profession

Still between Client
and Community

⚜

The contributions included in this issue of *Social Work* [September 1989] remind us of the vulnerabilities and the opportunities inherent in our profession's unique place, in the words of Bertha Reynolds, "Between client and community" (1934). Reynolds was not the first person to articulate this sentiment, but she was among the most eloquent voices to identify the profession's vulnerable position. She addressed social work's latent function of social control, criticizing the use of social services programs to co-opt the poor and to undermine and obviate any real momentum for major social change. It was Reynolds who asked the question: Whom do social workers serve when caught in a conflict between the interests of employers, governmental agencies, and the recipients of service? Also, she posed the profession's central dilemma when she wrote that the social work profession can serve both client and community and "preserve its integrity only if the processes of social change lead us to an organization of society in which the interests of all are safe-guarded through the participation of all in political and economic power" (1934, p. 126).

We have not attained a just society. In fact, despite the gains in social and economic participation achieved during the reform periods of the 1930s and the 1960s, the resource and power gaps continue to grow. The House of Representatives Ways and Means Committee has reported that Americans in the bottom one-fifth of income distribution suffered a 10 percent decline in real income from 1979 to 1987, whereas the income of Americans in the top one-fifth rose by 16 percent during the same period (Passell, 1989).

Furthermore, in the past eight years, we have witnessed a major dismantling of most social programs—a dismantling that has deprived a large segment of our population of needed economic, social, educational, and health services. Most shockingly, the average state-determined payment for Aid to Families with Dependent Children has been reduced by 25 percent. The symptoms of an unjust society, a society that excludes many from access to the opportunity structure, are all around us: homelessness, substance abuse, violence, and despair.

What happens to social workers who cherish Reynold's ideals as they attempt to serve clients in such a society? David Wagner in his fascinating article, "Fate of Idealism in Social Work: Alternative Experiences of Professional Careers" [pp. 389–395], explains the tension experienced and the career decisions made by a group of social workers who had been strongly committed to a radical political position and to social change. How have they fared in conservative America? These social workers were trying to function in an anomic situation, where there was disjunction between the goals they wished to achieve and the means available to them. Some of the social workers, as could be predicted, have left the profession. Others have abandoned their radical political and social goals and have become identified with their employing bureaucracies and, in fact, they have become critical and even disparaging of their own idealism. Also, some of the social workers have left unjust work environments to pursue their goals in other systems with clear political purpose. Reynolds resolved this dilemma for herself by accepting a position as a social worker in the Maritime Union, where her salary was paid by those whom she served.

Perhaps many social workers who are fleeing to private practice do so reluctantly—not out of a desire to be entrepreneurs or to abandon social work's professional mission—but to be free of the constraints of agency practice and to work for as well as with clients. Growing limitations imposed by insurance companies, however, are again demonstrating, as Reynolds knew so well, that "the one who pays the piper calls the tune."

Wagner, however, also found that many social workers are remaining in their tension-filled positions. They mediate their ideas through the profession and, out of a conviction that the personal is political, work for social change through the delivery of direct service to individuals, families, small groups, and communities.

But the stresses and pressures faced by social workers who continue to serve with integrity in an unjust society are great. Such social workers are caught between client and community and are constantly frustrated by forces that undermine their efforts at every turn. How is it that social workers often seem to be working against such odds with so little support? Why are their efforts so frequently criticized and disparaged? Poverty is not healthy for our society—nor is oppression, nor is neglect. Society will pay dearly for the destruction of people currently taking place in the inner cities and in the abandoned and impoverished rural areas.

In working with families, when a severely destructive problem persists and when family members, although requesting help, seem to fight any move toward change, a systemic practitioner may ask, "Does this family need this problem to maintain itself? How is this problem helping the family?" By analogy, as we struggle in our profession with forces that are impeding change for oppressed people, for troubled people, for people in poverty, we must ask these questions: Does our society need oppression and poverty? Does it need deviance to maintain stability? Does our society truly want us to enable oppressed and troubled people to move into the mainstream, to access opportunity, to share our resources, to share our lives?

As we consider the obstacles as we pursue social justice, it is enlightening to remember that many social scientists have speculated that our society requires poverty, oppression, and deviance. For example, Gans (1972) wrote about the positive functions of poverty. He pointed out that, among other things, the poor consume defective and damaged products at escalated prices, such as housing in disrepair or poor quality food and clothing. Piven and Cloward (1971) explained that a welfare system that is inaccessible or that simply maintains people in poverty provides an available force of poorly paid workers. Abramovitz (1988) has extended Piven and Cloward's analysis to demonstrate that our social policies, which are, after all, codified societal processes, have served to keep women at home or available for menial jobs only. Kai Erikson (1962) pointed out that deviance is necessary to mark and maintain social norms. He speculated that we need the example of oppressed and punished deviants to announce society's rules in a dramatic way and to construct an invisible social boundary that others hesitate to cross. Bowen's (1978) view was that our society uses discrimination and oppression in a massive scapegoating or societal projection process to absorb anxiety and project blame.

These theorists help us to consider why it is so difficult for social workers, working at the boundaries, to help people overcome their marginality and to become fully functional and rewarded members of their communities. Possibly, when we help people to improve their lives we are working against major regulatory processes in our society. This inconsistency is the fundamental dilemma. This dilemma is the vulnerability of our position between client and community.

However, it is just this position, our attention to person and situation and our refusal to retreat from mounting social problems by redefining them as personal defects, that creates the special character of social work. Such a position creates both dilemmas and opportunities. Most social workers are remaining in this stressful position, delivering direct service, subverting societal homeostatic processes through empowering clients and, as Wagner suggests, attempting "to create the preconditions for a new society on a micro-level through a series of personal transformations" (p. 392). When we consider our professional vision and the resulting inevitable dilemmas, it is not surprising that Arthur Dobrin in his article, "Ethical Judgments of Male and Female Social Workers," [pp. 451–455] concluded that social workers do not perceive abstract thinking about rights and justice and the ethics of responsibility and care to be incompatible. Social workers must relate to both justice and care every day!

Thus, my goal as editor-in-chief is to reaffirm the importance of maintaining our position between client and community. In this issue of *Social Work*, we learn about the value of our special perspective in child welfare and in occupational social work. In addition, we learn about social workers empowering developmentally disabled and mentally ill people by helping them gain mastery over their lives and competence in their environments. We learn about practitioners working with families on behalf of children in the schools. We learn more about our clients and potential clients—the blue-collar unemployed, caregiving spouses, the elderly Chinese—and we learn about their strengths and vision of what is truly helpful.

Social Work has several purposes: to bring to social workers useful knowledge, to provide a forum for the discussion of social and professional issues and dilemmas, and to present a variety of views of social workers at work. Perhaps, the overarching mission of *Social Work*—our major instrument for communication in the profession—is to tell ourselves about ourselves, to provide a discourse, which, through a circular process, reports on and, at the same time, constructs our professional identity.

Therefore, it is essential to the vitality of the profession that social workers from every segment of our varied professional world participate in this discourse and contribute to the ongoing social construction and reconstruction of our profession.

References

Abramovitz, M. (1988). *Regulating the lives of women*. Boston: South End Press.

Bowen, M. (1978). *Family therapy in clinical practice*. New York: J. Aronson

Erikson, K. T. (1962). Notes on the sociology of deviance. *Social Problems, 10*, 307–314.

Gans, H. (1972). The positive functions of poverty. *American Journal of Sociology, 78*, 275–289.

Passell, P. (1989, July 16). Forces in society in Reaganism, help dig deeper hole for poor [Economic watch]. *New York Times*, p. 1.

Piven, F. F., & Cloward, R. A. (1971). *Regulating the poor: The functions of public welfare*. New York: Pantheon.

Reynolds, B. C. (1934). Between client and community: A study in responsibility in social casework. *Smith College Studies in Social Work Monographs, 5*(1), 5–128.

First published September 1989

A Profession Chasing Its Tail–Again

I t was with sadness, anger, disappointment, and confusion that social workers learned of the breakdown of the hard-won collaboration between the National Association of Social Workers and the National Registry of Health Care Providers in Clinical Social Work. That collaboration had established the American Board of Examiners in Clinical Social Work and a single advanced credential for clinical social workers.

It was also disturbing to learn that this painful and difficult rupture has ended up in the courts. Let us hope that we do not have ahead of us a long and costly legal battle—because no one would win but the lawyers. Sure to lose would be the profession. Sure to lose would be the average clinical social worker who has been trying to understand and act responsibly in the face of the complexities of credentialing.

First, what is it all about? Probably no one can fully understand at this point all of the actions and reactions, the beliefs and disappointments, the aspirations and agendas that have played a part in this failed effort. Complex, conflictual, and competitive transactional processes take on a life of their own. They become "runaways" or deviation-amplifying feedback processes that are out of control. Perhaps it would be helpful to stand back, take a long view, and at least understand the historical context that provided fertile soil for conflict and distrust.

Almost four years ago it became evident that, in the move toward advanced credentialing in clinical social work, our profession was going to have two separate but very similar advanced clinical credentials. To avoid this and for the sake of the profession, the leaders of the National Registry, the National Federation of Societies for Clinical Social Work, and NASW came together to explore the possibility of a single credentialing process for advanced clinical practice.

In October 1986, negotiating teams appointed by NASW and the National Registry, a group with ideological ties to the Societies for Clinical Social Work, began their work. For many, whether or not they felt advanced credentialing was useful or necessary, this negotiating process opened the door for the resolution of some long-unsolved issues. Issues could now be revisited that had burdened the profession since the American Association of Psychiatric Social Workers (AAPSW) joined with other specialty groups and the more generic organization, the American Association of Social Workers (AASW), to found NASW 35 years ago. Coming together in a single organization was an enormous achievement for our profession. However, it did not resolve all of the differences between the varied groups that came under the umbrella of the new organization. Struggling to build cohesion, NASW tended to focus on what was shared and common among all social workers. Many of the specialist groups felt that their interests were lost in the attempt to meet the needs of such a widely diverse profession. In a sense, the attempts to organize played out on an institutional level an age-old theme in our identity struggles, the tension between generic and specific visions of the profession.

When NASW was barely a decade old, many social workers' priorities turned to the war on poverty, the crisis in the cities, civil rights, and social change, and direct practice was often undervalued or disparaged. Some clinical social workers began to feel that NASW was not a supportive professional or collegial environment in which to pursue their interests and goals, and Societies of Clinical Social Work began to develop in the various states. In some respects, these groups inherited the traditions of AAPSW. Other specialty groups began to develop, and social workers, in their adaptable and pragmatic way, chose between organizations or more often were members of both the specialty organization and NASW.

In the past decade, the rapidly growing NASW has worked hard to respond to the needs of the various groups through the specialty conferences and through the development of the commissions focusing on the different fields of practice. The association was particularly attentive to disaffected clinical social workers through offering several special conferences, a registry service, and vigorous and successful action to promote licensing and vendorship. The state Societies of Clinical Social Work also grew rapidly and federated into a national organization. The result was two different and parallel organizational structures serving the needs of clinical social workers.

As the negotiating teams brought together people from the different traditions, old and new questions emerged: Is clinical social work defined by a specific field of practice, that is, mental health? Or is it an approach, a perspective, a method that is in some sense generic, that could be carried into any setting? And how should it be defined? An outstanding achievement of the negotiating group was the adoption of a definition of clinical social work. A variety of contentious political issues also emerged, because each organization had to voluntarily relinquish power to establish a free-standing accrediting body. It is a testimony to the patience, tenacity, creativity, and diplomacy of the members of the negotiating teams that by October 1987 a memorandum of agreement was achieved. It also demonstrated the commitment of the organizations involved to the welfare of the profession that the memorandum was accepted by each organization and ABE came into being.

Clearly, all of the issues were not fully resolved, and none of the actors was totally satisfied. That is the nature of a true compromise; it is acceptable to all parties but does not fulfill anyone's complete agenda. Despite this, most experienced a sense of accomplishment and were relieved that the two organizations had come together and made significant progress toward building linkages and collaboration. People were encouraged that a single advanced clinical credentialing process would be in place and that the profession would be strengthened and advanced in an atmosphere of cooperation.

Within two years, the hopes for such collaboration were dashed. What happened? Perhaps eventually the nature and causes of the difficulties will become clear. What is clear now is widespread disappointment and frustration that this important joint venture has foundered. Once again, our profession has failed to manage conflict well.

But this is not the first time we have found ourselves caught in conflict. Over the years our profession has involved itself in a series of embittered ideological and political struggles. Just a few examples may be recalled. In our professional infancy, when we were struggling to define ourselves, we were faced with a bitter and public conflict between our two most valued fore-mothers, Jane Addams and Mary Richmond, each of whom had very different views of social work.

The 1930s saw the continuation of the Addams–Richmond struggles in the battles between Mary Van Kleek, representing radical social change, and Grace Marcus, the inheritor of the Charity Organization Society and the Richmond tradition. In the 1940s, one of the most talented and respected leaders, Bertha Reynolds, was quietly excluded from the profession because of her political and social philosophy.

One of the most destructive ideological battles lasted from the mid-1930s well into the 1960s between the Functionalists, followers of Otto Rank, and those who followed Freud, members of the Diagnostic School. This ideological controversy totally split the direct-service arm of the profession and forced students, workers, agencies, and schools to choose sides: an either-or ideological battle. Although nuances of this almost religious conflict echo today, most modern practitioners incorporate, without even knowing it, principles from both supposedly irreconcilable theoretical positions.

In the 1960s, it was direct practice—casework—that was on the block as many of those who favored social change and community action found it necessary to disparage the value of what Richmond had called "the retail method." We found ourselves broadcasting to the world that what most of us did in our daily work "didn't work."

This recent struggle between NASW and ABE is not our first political battle. In fact, the long history of divisiveness and suspicion between practitioners and educators is exemplified in the fact that our major professional organization and our accrediting body are separate. Two years ago, negotiating teams were established by the Council on Social Work Education and

NASW to examine the possibility of closer liaison, collaboration, and mutual support. That formal negotiating effort lasted for one painful meeting. However—and perhaps this can be a model for the current situation—following the rupture of formal negotiations, each organization reached out to reestablish informal dialogue and to form linkages. Regular contact and meetings have been established, and closer collaboration between the two organizations is becoming a reality.

But what is it about our profession? Why do we have such trouble with conflict, with difference? We should be excellent communicators, skilled listeners, expert negotiators. We are firm believers in the value and dignity of each person and are strong advocates for self-determination. These skills and values direct our work with clients. How is it that so often they don't get carried over into our work with each other?

Why do we so often try to gain recognition and validation of our various ideological positions or approaches to practice by attacking the views and visions of others? Why can't we be secure enough in our identity as a profession to validate and even welcome different views, different approaches, different sets of priorities? Why is it that our political and turf battles become so bitter? Is it because when resources are scarce, competition intensifies? Or is it, as someone once said about academia, that the conflicts are intense because the stakes are so small?

Social work frequently comes under attack. During conservative political periods, our programs are cut, our goals are derided, our motives questioned. Let us not respond to attacks from the outside by attacking each other. Let us not, like F Troop, flail around and knock each other down.

Under the umbrella of social work, a large and diverse group of professionals works in many different ways to help others, to administer service delivery systems, to bring about social change. Let us air and argue our differences in an atmosphere of respect and open-mindedness, let us negotiate and collaborate around issues of power and turf, and let us share our limited resources. Most important, let us keep the welfare of our clients our most important priority.

First published March 1990

Social Worker–in–Situation

Social work has long been characterized by its particular perspective on the person-in-situation. Focusing on the complex transactions between the human being and the ecological environment, the profession's mission is to improve the quality of life of its clients, enhance social functioning, and intervene to make the environment on all levels more supportive and enabling. This perspective is not only valuable in understanding and helping clients; it can also illuminate aspects of our lives as social workers.

Social work practice has always been rooted in agencies and organizations, and the authors in this issue [May 1991] seek to discover how workers are faring in these organizations. Their findings are disquieting.

Although the authors focus on different kinds of settings and organizations, common themes emerge. Stress and burnout appear to be ubiquitous to agency practice or practice within service organizations. In fact, Srinika Jayaratne, Mary Lou Davis-Sacks, and Wayne A. Chess [pp. 224–229] found that workers in private practice fare better than those in agency practice.

What, then, has happened to agency practice? Each of the authors explores the social worker's experience at work and the sources of strain within agencies and organizations. Stressful conditions in the workplace appear to be particularly destructive to the practitioner's work life. One is the loss of autonomy that is increasingly experienced by workers in agency practice. This erosion of autonomy is a result of many factors. The increased bureaucratization of social welfare organizations, the hierarchical organizational styles borrowed from the business world, and the employment of business-trained bureaucrats to administer social services agencies tends to develop a working situation that sharply limits the autonomy and creativity of line workers, burying them in record keeping and other administrative procedures. This type of organizational structure is inimical to the styles and values of social workers and, as Patricia L. Ewalt [pp. 214–217] suggests, of women. As Joan Arches [pp. 202–206] reminds us, 30 years ago Litwak (1961) described the kind of organizational structure that promoted the performance of nonroutine tasks as nonhierarchical, nonbureaucratic, participatory, nonspecialized, and with a minimum of rules and procedures. This, of course, is the opposite of the organizational patterns increasingly in place in social agencies and other service organizations.

Professional social work practice is an individualizing process. Our expertise is to respond differentially to the individual "case," whether it be of an individual, family, group, or community, keeping in mind its uniqueness and particular characteristics. If the constraints of bureaucracy push us into a routinized practice that treats different situations as if they were the same, we have abandoned one of our major missions and skills.

Worker autonomy has also been sharply limited by the increasing control by funding sources in defining the nature of practice. Most of the writers express concern about this distortion of accountability and about the fact that the requirements of the funding sources and concern about the bottom line are dominating the decision-making process, not only programmatically but in the handling of individual cases. The pressure is often on workers to do more with less or, eventually, to do less with less, to process the maximum number of people in the shortest possible time. Professional judgment concerning client need and appropriate responses to need are overridden by financial and bureaucratic requirements.

Closely related to the loss of autonomy is the fact that social workers are often finding themselves in situations where their values and the values of their profession are in conflict with those of the organizations within which they work. Naturally, the less autonomy practitioners have, the more unable they are to translate their values into action.

These trends in social agencies and other service organizations must, of course, be understood in the larger social, political, and economic contexts. The work that social workers do is not valued by our society. The destruction of social programs, the transfer of resources away from the poor, the shift of financial support from social to military causes, the fact that we live not in a gentler, kinder society but in one that is leaner and meaner, profoundly affect the systems within which social workers work.

It is not surprising that the past decade has seen growing concern about and studies of social workers in the workplace, with considerable focus on burnout. "Burnout" has been defined by Arches as "a cluster of physical, emotional, and interactional symptoms related to job stress and includes emotional exhaustion, a sense of lacking personal accomplishment, and depersonalization of clients." According to researchers, it may include a range of physical symptoms, poor self-esteem, substance abuse, withdrawal, and a tendency to blame clients for their problems (Cherniss, 1980).

How can we understand the impact of the work situation on the social worker? What psychosocial theories can illuminate the dynamics of this complex interaction? Two bodies of thought that provided conceptual support for the social reform movements and the innovative service delivery strategies of the 1960s and early 1970s can be called on to clarify the linkage between loss of autonomy and unresolvable value dilemmas and the responses of professional social workers to these stressful conditions. The first theory, developed by psychologist Robert White (1959) and translated into practice by Gladwin (1967), Germain (1981), and Maluccio (1981), posits that all human beings have an inborn need to experience themselves as a cause and to interact effectively with the environment. Not experiencing oneself as effective leads to feelings of incompetence and to low self-esteem. Social workers in situations where the constraints and limitations are oppressive, where resources are limited, and where autonomy is sharply curtailed do not have an opportunity to be effective, to be a cause, to make things happen. They do not have an opportunity for personal accomplishment. After all, what is work all about? It is about competently and effectively having an impact on the environment; it is about making a difference. If our work situations do not make this possible, the result is frustration and, eventually, alienation from a self-defeating environment.

Anomie theory is a second body of thought that can illuminate the relationship between the worker and the workplace. Developed by Durkheim (1897) almost a century ago and expanded by sociologist Robert Merton (1957), anomie, in its modern dress as "opportunity theory" (Cloward & Ohlin, 1960), became a major plank in the conceptual platform that supported the War on Poverty program. An anomic situation is one in which cherished and accepted goals cannot be achieved by the institutional means or norms available. It is possible that many social workers are working in anomic situations in that their goals of helping clients cannot be achieved by the means available or within the constraints of agency norms. Merton has pointed out that in such a situation four adaptations are available.

First, a social worker employed in a setting where he or she cannot help clients within agency norms and means may adopt a ritualized adaptation, abandoning the goals and aimlessly performing the prescribed but ineffective tasks. This adaptation tends to lead to depersonalization of the client, as described in the burnout literature. Second, the worker may adopt an innovative solution, clinging to the goals but moving outside of the structure and the norms of the agency to help the client. Such a position is highly stressful for the worker, who is violating agency procedures or investing himself or herself far and above the call of duty. This adaptation cannot last; the innovator either gets into trouble with the administration or becomes totally spent. Anomie theory suggests that the defeated and exhausted worker moves to one of the other three adaptations to the anomic situation.

The third adaptation, retreatism, involves the relinquishment of both the goals and the norms of the system, either through withdrawal and alienation on the job or through leaving the setting to find another situation where the goals and the means for attaining them are better integrated. It is possible that many social workers are finding private practice that kind of opportunity. The final response to the anomic situation as described by Merton is rebellion. Rebellion involves active effort to challenge goals, norms, and means and to bring about social change so that the approved goals may be achieved through the means and norms of the organization.

We welcome the examination of agency and institutional settings in furthering our understanding of worker stress and burnout. We have, perhaps, focused too much on worker and client characteristics. Esposito and Fine (1985) suggested that

> the burnout ideology fosters the notion that workers are burned out from clients, too much work, or the stresses of human services . . . / . . . camouflaging systems problems. Cast as a personal and personnel issue, rather than a collective and structural issue, this ideology preserves the illusion that all is well in the agency and the world around it. (pp. 737–738)

In the studies of social worker-in-situation published in this issue, this illusion is challenged. The enthusiasm, energy, and satisfaction so apparent in the Family Preservation Movement are a useful illustration. These child welfare practitioners, working with some of the most challenging families in the social welfare system, are finding satisfaction and a sense of being effective, creative, and autonomous—of making a difference—because they are given the time and the resources to do the job. Are these not the same workers who have suffered so from burnout? Are these not the same difficult and despairing families that overwhelm child welfare workers with feelings of hopelessness and helplessness? The difference is the context of the work.

This small but very successful revolution in child welfare communicates a powerful message to us all. Social workers can do the tough jobs and want to do the tough jobs if they are in a situation where they have what they need to do the job and to do it right.

References

Cherniss, C. (1980). *Staff burnout. Job stress in the human services.* Beverly Hills, CA: Sage Publications.

Cloward, R. A., & Ohlin, L. E. (1960). *Delinquency and opportunity.* New York: Free Press.

Durkheim, E. (1897). *Le suicide: Etude de sociologie*. Paris: Felix Alcan.

Esposito, G., & Fine, M. (1985). The field of child welfare as a world of work. In A. Laird & A. Hartman (Eds.), *A handbook of child welfare*. New York: Free Press.

Germain, C. B. (1981). An ecological approach to people–environmental transactions. *Social Casework, 62,* 323–331.

Gladwin, T. (1967). Social competence and clinical practice. *Psychiatry, 30,* 30–43.

Litwak, E. (1961). Models of bureaucracy that permit conflict. *American Journal of Sociology, 67,* 177–184.

Maluccio, A. N. (Ed.). (1981). *Promoting (competence in clients—A new/old approach to social work practice*. New York: Free Press.

Merton, R. (1957). *Social theory and social structure*. Glencoe, IL: Free Press.

White, R. (1959). Motivation reconsidered: The concept of competence. *Psychological Review, 66,* 297–333.

First published March 1990

The Professional Is Political

I understood from the teachers in those segregated schools that the work of any teacher committed to the full self-realization of students was necessarily and fundamentally radical, that ideas were not neutral, that to teach in a way that liberates, that expands consciousness, that awakens, is to challenge domination at its very core.
—bell hooks, 1989, p. 50

For almost two decades, empowerment has been enthusiastically embraced as a highly valued goal of social work practice. Sparked by the publication of Barbara Solomon's (1976) *Black Empowerment: Social Work in Oppressed Communities*, "empowerment" became the primary stated objective in practice with disadvantaged and oppressed groups. The social work literature was replete with articles extolling the empowerment of clients through social work practice. In fact, empowerment has been assumed to be a part of most practice.

As we have embraced this ideal, it may be that we have not really examined the dilemmas that emerge and the choices to be made when a profession adopts empowerment as a mission. It may be that empowerment exists more in our professional discourse than in actual practice. There are many forces—institutional, economic, political, ideological, and historical—that continue to be obstacles to the achievement of a truly empowering practice.

The dilemmas implicit in a profession's commitment to client empowerment are not new. These dilemmas have challenged the profession, although perhaps in different words, since we attempted to separate ourselves from our early beginnings rooted in moral superiority, noblesse oblige, and social control.

The profession attempted that separation by adopting the value of client self-determination, the precursor to empowerment. *Self-determination* was defined as the clients' right to make their own choices, to define their own destiny. But for many, self-determination was a hollow promise sharply limited by lack of access to resources, to opportunity, to power. Self-determination, colored by American individualism, was too often simply the right to be left alone. "Social workers' ability to put the principle of self-determination into practice . . . is affected and determined by the level of exploitation, oppression, and lack of available opportunities that clients confront" (Freedberg, 1989, p. 34). These limitations challenged social workers to turn to social action, to advocacy, and eventually to client empowerment so that inequalities could be addressed, opportunities made available, and client self-determination realized.

The language of empowerment has added new dimensions to self-determination. It envisions a more vigorous, more active stance. It implies that people have not only the right to self-determination, but also the right to the power, ability, and authority to achieve self-determination. "The ability to act in behalf of oneself is a function of factors such as critical consciousness, sense of entitlement, knowledge, resources, competency, skills, and self-respect" (Staples, 1990, p. 33).

In the discourse on empowerment, we have primarily focused on the oppression, marginalization, deprivation, and disempowerment of clients by large social forces, by society, by "the system." We have rarely examined the power dynamics as they exist in the worker–client relationship (Pinderhughes, 1989). We have been less ready to own that we, as professionals, are part of "the system" and to examine the implications of our position of power. We have been reluctant to speculate that perhaps if our clients are to truly become empowered, we must learn to shed some power (Hoffman, 1985).

Sources of Power

Perhaps the average social worker, constrained by resource limitations, policies, time, knowledge, and skill deficits, does not experience herself or himself as powerful, but in the worker–client relationship, in our accustomed models of professional practice, the power belongs to us. We attempt to constrain that power through contracting, respecting confidentiality, and attending to the principle of self-determination, but these efforts do not shift much of our power to the client. What, then, are the sources of our power? How can we share this power or divest ourselves of it to empower clients?

Agency Resources

First, in the case of agency- or institution-based practice, a source of social workers' power is "the resources and services controlled by the organization and agency in which they are employed" (Hasenfeld, 1987, p. 470). Sharing this power with clients entails a major reorganization of service delivery systems. Such radical reorganization would include giving clients greater control over the fiscal resources of the agency, the organization of clients into advocacy groups so that agencies would have to deal with clients as a collectivity in distributing resources and shaping programs, and finally the breakup of agency monopoly over services through the creation of client- and community-shaped alternative programs.

Examples of power sharing, client–consumer advocacy, and alternative programs do exist and clearly level the playing field on which the worker and the client meet, but for the most part agencies and institutions have been reluctant to relinquish control and continue to be hierarchically structured, with the client in the position of least power.

Expert Knowledge

A second source of professional power is the possession, privileging, and use of expert knowledge (Hartman, 1992). The privileging of the worker's knowledge in the helping professions has been intensified as those relationships have taken their "form from the expert–patient, diagnosis–treatment model that made medication a lucrative and highly prestigious profession" (Rappoport, Reischl, & Zimmerman, 1992, p. 84). In our drive for professionalization, we have replaced moral superiority with professional expertise and preserved our power to define the client, the reality, and the therapy. This "furnishes the client a lesson in inferiority" (Gergen & Kaye, 1992, p. 171). We have been reluctant to "let the client be the ultimate source of authority in his own affairs" (Reynolds, 1934, p. 35).

Current challenges to the medical–expert clinical model have emerged. One is the "strengths perspective" in social work, which is based on discovering the power within people. Saleebey (1992) observed:

> To discover that power, we must subvert and abjure pejorative labels, provide opportunities for connection to family, institution, and community, assail the victim mindset, foreswear paternalism (even in its most benign guises) and trust people's intuitions, accounts, perspectives, and energies. (p. 8)

A second is the continuing challenge of social group work, which was founded in a more collaborative, empowering tradition and was less influenced by professionalization and medicalization. Group workers have been revisiting and reclaiming their heritage and tapping the empowerment potential of mutual aid, self-help, and shared purpose (Lee, 1988).

In the individual and family therapy fields, social constructionist thinkers have been challenging the privileging of professional expertise; adopting a stance of uncertainty, curiosity, and discovery; tolerating ambiguity and confusion; and searching for indigenous knowledge (Amundson, Stewart, & Valentine, 1993).

The surfacing and crediting of the client's knowledge and experience is central in all empowering practice and has been key in the development of models in which verbal and written expression are encouraged, in which those who have been silenced claim their voices (Nelson, 1991). As bell hooks (1989) phrased it,

> Moving from silence into speech is for the oppressed, the colonized, the exploited, and those who stand and struggle side by side, a gesture of defiance that heals, that makes new life and new growth possible. It is that act of speech, of "talking back," that is no mere ges-

ture of empty words, that is the expression of our movement from object to subject—the liberated voice. (p. 9)

We must relinquish the role of expert so that our client narratives and experiences can be validated (Tobias, 1990). We do not discard our knowledge; we cease to privilege it, we apply our knowledge with caution and humility, with the recognition that it is one of many "truths," with the awareness that it is a social construction and that the "social group that defines the problems, concepts, assumptions, and hypotheses in a field leaves its 'social fingerprints' on the image that emerges" (Swigonski, 1993, p. 179). We must be on the alert to identify those social fingerprints.

Interpersonal Power

A third source of our power is that which is gained through the ability to persuade. This develops not only out of the role of expert but also from our role as helper and our interpersonal skills, particularly the ability to develop empathy, trust, and rapport with the client (Hasenfeld, 1987). This power is greatly accentuated through the development of transference in some models of practice and through the use of paradoxical injunctions, mysterious messages, and other powerful strategies in other models.

If we are serious about the empowerment of clients, we must question approaches that increase the power of the social worker in the treatment situation. What can be the nature of a worker–client relationship that will provide a level playing field for the work? A client-empowering relationship is collaborative and egalitarian, open and sharing. The effort is to keep transference to a minimum and to foster independence, competence, strengths, and confidence. The empowering relationship can perhaps best be described as a partnership.

Legitimate Power

A fourth source of power is legitimate power—the power legally invested in social workers to perform certain functions of social control. For example, we have, as a profession, been charged to intervene to protect children and elders in situations of abuse and neglect. These and other legitimized social control functions have been a part of our professional sanction and clearly limit our adherence to the principle of self-determination. Some have felt that the social control functions are inappropriate for a profession committed to social change, social justice, and empowerment.

In situations in which social workers are legitimately empowered to act with authority, they must possess power and of necessity will limit client self-determination, intervening to interrupt or to prevent behavior that has been defined as antisocial. We must not shirk our protective responsibility, but we also must not expand it. We must be clear about what legitimate power is and what its limits are, and we must not extend our professional influence to support dominant cultural values and norms beyond these limits. When we do surpass our legitimate power, we become the arbiters of the dominant culture and instruments of illegitimate social control, not unlike our forebears. Our role in empowerment practice is to open up options, to help clients expand their choices, or to help them become free to consider multiple paths.

Choosing Our Power

All social workers deal with issues of power. The choices we make concerning how to deal with our power and our agency's power are crucial. We may choose to keep our power and use it in behalf of clients, or we may choose to work on policy, agency, and interpersonal levels to transfer power to clients.

This is not a trivial choice, for to take the second option commits one to radical change in service delivery systems and in our practice.

References

Amundson, J., Stewart, K., & Valentine, L. (1993). Temptations of power and certainty. *Journal of Marital and Family Therapy, 19*(2), 111–123.

Freedberg, S. (1989). Self-determination: Historical perspectives and effects on current practice. *Social Work, 34,* 33–38.

Gergen, K. J., & Kaye, J. (1992). Beyond narrative in the negotiation of therapeutic meaning. In S. McNamee & K. J.

Gergen (Eds.), *Therapy as social construction*. London: Sage Publications.

Hartman, A. (1992). In search of subjugated knowledge. *Social Work, 37*, 483–484.

Hasenfeld, Y. (1987). Power in social work practice. *Social Service Review, 61*(3), 469–483.

Hoffman, L (1985). Beyond power and control: Toward a "second order" family systems therapy. *Family Systems Medicine, 3*, 381–395.

hooks, b. (1989). *Talking back: Thinking feminist: Thinking black*. Boston: South End Press.

Lee, J. (Ed.). (1988). Group work with the oppressed [Special issue]. *Social Work with Groups, 11*(4), 1–139.

Nelson, M. (1991). Empowerment of incest survivors: Speaking out. *Families in Society, 72*(10), 618–624.

Pinderhughes, E. (1989). *Understanding race, ethnicity, and power*. New York: Free Press.

Rappoport, J., Reischl, T., & Zimmerman, M. (1992). Mutual help mechanisms in the empowerment of former mental patients. In D. Saleebey (Ed.), *The strengths perspective in social work practice* (pp. 84–97). New York: Longman.

Reynolds, B. C. (1934). Between client and community: A study in responsibility in social casework. *Smith College Studies in Social Work, 5*(1), 5–128.

Saleebey, D. (1992). Introduction: Power in the people. In D. Saleebey (Ed.), *The strengths perspective in social work practice* (pp. 3–17). New York: Longman.

Solomon, B. (1976). *Black empowerment: Social work in oppressed communities*. New York: Columbia University Press.

Staples, L. (1990). Powerful ideas about empowerment. *Administration in Social Work, 14*(2), 29–42.

Swigonski, M. E. (1993). Feminist standpoint theory and the questions of social work research. *Affilia, 8*(2), 171–183.

Tobias, M. (1990). Validator: A key role in empowering the chronically mentally ill. *Social Work, 35*, 357–359.

First published July 1993

Index

A

Abortion, 103–107
Adoption Assistance and Child
  Welfare Act of 1980, 144
Agency practice
  AIDS work in, 98–99, 100
  dynamics of power in, 173
  organizational structure, 165–166
  stress in, 165–166, 168–169
Aging
  caretaking trends, 31–34
  demographic trends, 31, 32
AIDS, 97–101
Aid to Families with Dependent
  Children, 118–120, 154
American Association of Psychiatric
  Social Workers, 160
American Association of Social
  Workers, 160
American Board of Examiners in
  Clinical Social Work, 159–161,
  162–163
Anomie theory, 51–52, 168–169
Arms control, 68–69
Assessment
  biological perspective, 18
  of homelessness effects, 92, 94
  narrative accounts in, 19
  religious/spiritual values in,
  17–18
  sociopolitical context, 23–25
  trends, 19

B

Biological perspective, 18
Bowers v. Hardwick, 58
Braschi v. Stahl Associates, 139–140
Burger, Chief Justice Warren, 56
Burnout, 167–169

Bush administration, 32–33, 45,
  50–51, 52–53, 81–82
  family services in, 35, 141, 143
  Persian Gulf War, 71

C

Caretaking responsibility, social
  trends in, 33–35
Child abuse
  child's account of, 127
  family preservation programs and,
  143, 148
  social perception of, 124–125
Child services
  AIDS and, 99
  family preservation programs,
  144–149, 169
  need for, 119
  public attitude toward, 117–120
  in Reagan administration,
  118–119
  social work in, 120–121
Cities, 49–50
Civil rights movements
  gay liberation, 55–57
  as insurrection of subjugated
  knowledge, 25–26
Clinton administration, 55
  in construction of national
  narrative, 86–88
  goals of, 85–86, 88
  hopes for, 79–83
Credentialing issues, 159–163

D

Deinstitutionalization, 93
*Diagnostic and Statistical Manual of
  Mental Disorders,* 24
Diversity, as social value, 80–81

E
Economic issues
  goals of Clinton administration,
    85–86
  health care spending, 109,
    110–112, 113
  opportunity structure, 50–52, 53
  poverty in America, 49–50
  role of social work in, 52–54
  single-parent households, 134
  support for child services,
    118–119
  tax structure, 53, 80, 86, 118,
    141
  women and poverty, 31–32, 34
Education, campus free-speech
  issues, 37–41
Empowerment of client
  diagnostic practice and, 24–25
  free speech and, 39–40
  as goal of social work, 171–172
  knowledge systems and, 23–24,
    27
  role of social work, 25–27
  social work as institutional power
    and, 172–176

F
Families
  caretaking responsibility, 33–35
  defining, 132–134, 139–141
  demographic trends, 132–133
  family planning, 107
  family preservation programs,
    143–149, 169
  family values controversy,
    137–139
  single-parent, 134
  in social work practice, 131,
    133–136
  violence in, 123–129
Family Leave Act, 141
Family Preservation and Child
  Welfare Reform Act, 143–144,
  145
Foster care, 145
Foucalt, M., 23, 24, 25, 39

Free speech
  harassment of minorities and,
    37–38, 39–40
  postmodernist thought and,
    39–40

G
Great Society, 51–52
Group work, 174

H
Harris v. McRae, 104
Health care reform, 81
  access issues in, 112–114
  family-planning provisions in,
    107
  government involvement,
    110–111
  impetus for, 109–110
  privatization in, 111
  reimbursement systems in,
    111–112
  resource allocation decisions,
    113–114
  role of social work in, 112, 114
Health issues
  aging of population, 32–33
  AIDS, 97–101
  right to death, 110
Hill, Anita, 43–46, 80
Homelessness, 91–95
  avoidant responses to, 91–92
  causes of, 92–93
  empathy in assessment of, 92
  legislation, 92
  public response to, 93–94, 95
  social work response to, 94–95
Homosexuality
  assessment of, 24
  civil rights movement, 25
  gay liberation movement, 56–58,
    60–61
  homophobic violence, 59
  in legislation, 58–59, 141
  military service and, 55–56
  social work in gay rights
    movement, 60–61

I

Immigration
  role of social work in, 69
  U.S. legislation, 67
International affairs
  concern for children in, 117, 120
  Persian Gulf War, 71–75
  social work and, 66–70
  U.S. role in, 65–66

K

Karger, H. J., 12–13

L

Language
  of family violence, 127, 128
  meaning-formulation in, 73–74
Legislation
  abortion, 103–104
  child services in, 118–119, 121
  definition of family in, 133,
    139–140
  family services, 141, 143–146,
    148
  gay rights, 58–59
  homelessness, 92
  immigration, 67
  spouse abuse in, 126
Los Angeles, after Rodney King
  verdict, 49–54

M

Media, Persian Gulf War coverage,
  71–73, 74
Mental illness, homelessness and, 92
Military social work, 75

N

Narrative construction
  in civil rights movements, 25–26
  at national level, 86–88
  political power and, in Persian
    Gulf War, 73–74
  professional knowledge base and,
    14–15, 17, 27
  in social work assessment, 19
National Association of Social
  Workers, 159–163

National Federation of Societies for
  Clinical Social Work, 160
National Registry of Health Care
  Providers in Clinical Social Work,
  159–163

P

Patient's rights, 25
Persian Gulf War, 71–75, 127–128
Person-in-situation perspective, 165,
  169
Political correctness debate, 54
  free-speech issues in, 37–40
  social work in, 40–41
Political power
  citizen influence, 81–83
  citizen perception of, 79–80
  gay liberation and, 56
  narrative construction and, 73–74
  role of social work and, 153–157
  social control function of social
    work, 175–176
  social work activism, 53
  special interests in, 81
  women's, 45, 47
Postmodernism, 39–40
Privacy rights, 103–104, 107
Professional development
  advocacy in, 123–124, 153–157
  client empowerment and, 27,
    173–175
  credentialing, 159, 161
  family preservation programs,
    144–149, 169
  family services, 131, 133–136
  impact of AIDS, 97–101
  professional associations, 159–163
  professional epistemology, 19–20
  in response to homelessness,
    94–95
  role of research in, 12–13
  social context of, 20
  social worker stress, 165–169
  sources of knowing in, 13–15, 17
Public opinion
  1992 election, 85
  abortion rights, 106–107

perception of family violence,
123–126, 127
public care for children, 119–120
trust of government, 79–80

Q

Quayle, Dan, 137, 138–139

R

Racism/racial bias, 52
campus free-speech codes and,
37, 39–40
caretaking role and, 34
social work role in combating,
53–54
Reagan administration, 32–33, 50,
51
family services in, 141, 145
health care system in, 110
housing access and, 93
status of children in, 118–119
Religion/spirituality, 17–18
Research
client as collaborator in, 25–27
empirical testing, 11
needs, 13–15
professional development and,
12–13
Roe v. Wade, 103–104
Rust v. Sullivan, 104

S

Sanders, Daniel, 69–70
Schindler, Allen, 55–56
Sexual abuse, 127
Sexual harassment
role of social work in countering,
47
Thomas–Hill controversy, 43–47
Social work education
AIDS and, 98, 99, 100
credentialing issues, 159, 161
gay rights and, 60

liberal arts education and, 41
Social Work journal, editorial
practices, 5–7, 13, 20–21, 157
Spouse abuse
social perception of, 123–124,
125–126
social work and, 125–127
Stewart B. McKinney Homeless
Assistance Act of 1987, 92
Substance abuse, 52

T

Tax system, 53, 80, 86, 118, 141
Thomas, Clarence, Supreme Court
nomination of, 43–46, 80

U

United Nations, 68, 120

V

Violence/violent behavior
anti-homosexual, 59
in families, 123–129

W

War, social work and, 75
War on Poverty, 50–51, 168
Widowhood, 31–32
Women's issues, 24, 25
abortion, 103–107
aging as, 31–35
caretaking responsibility, 33–35
feminization of poverty, 31–32
political representation, 45, 47
sexual harassment, 45–47
spouse abuse, 123–124, 125–126
Workplace issues
family structure and, 133–134
in social work settings, 165–169
women and poverty, 32, 34

Z

Zaniecki, Florian, 12

The NASW Press
Brings It All Together for You

Reflection & Controversy: Essays on Social Work, *by Ann Hartman (with a foreword by Carel B. Germain).* Chronicles the social and political evolution of social work between September 1989 and November 1993. Provocative, insightful, and sometimes controversial, this book is classic Hartman—certain to stimulate lively discussion and critical thinking. **$18.95**

Social Work Speaks: NASW Policy Statements, 3rd edition. This unabridged collection of policy statements adopted by the National Association of Social Workers (NASW) reflects "the collective voice of social work." Ratified by the NASW Delegate Assembly, a group of 300 elected social work professionals from all fields of practice. **$28.95**

Research on Children *edited by Shirley Buttrick.* A collection of essays, originally published in the March 1992 edition of *Social Work Research & Abstracts,* reissued in book form to meet overwhelming reader demand. Articles address foster care, adoption, mental health, child care, and other critical aspects of child welfare. **$12.95**

(order form on back)

The NASW Press
Brings It All Together for You

Reflection & Controversy: Essays on Social Work, *by Ann Hartman (with a foreword by Carel B. Germain).* Chronicles the social and political evolution of social work between September 1989 and November 1993. Provocative, insightful, and sometimes controversial, this book is classic Hartman—certain to stimulate lively discussion and critical thinking. **$18.95**

Social Work Speaks: NASW Policy Statements, 3rd edition. This unabridged collection of policy statements adopted by the National Association of Social Workers (NASW) reflects "the collective voice of social work." Ratified by the NASW Delegate Assembly, a group of 300 elected social work professionals from all fields of practice. **$28.95**

Research on Children *edited by Shirley Buttrick.* A collection of essays, originally published in the March 1992 edition of *Social Work Research & Abstracts,* reissued in book form to meet overwhelming reader demand. Articles address foster care, adoption, mental health, child care, and other critical aspects of child welfare. **$12.95**

(order form on back)

ORDER FORM

Title	Item #	Price	Total
Reflection & Controversy	**Item 2332**	**$18.95**	_____
Social Work Speaks	Item 2340	$28.95	_____
Research on Children	Item 2235	$12.95	_____

+ 10% postage and handling _____

Total _____

☐ I've enclosed my check or money order for $ _____

☐ Please charge my   ☐ NASW Visa   ☐ Other Visa   ☐ MasterCard

  Credit Card No._____Exp. Date_____

  Signature _____

Name _____

Address _____

City_____State_____Zip_____

(Make checks payable to NASW Press.) Prices are subject to change.

NASW Distribution Center   Credit card orders call **1-800-227-3590**

P.O. Box 431   (In metro DC, call 301-317-8688)

Annapolis JCT, MD 20701   NASW PRESS   Or fax your order to **301-206-7989**

*RC 1/94

ORDER FORM

Title	Item #	Price	Total
Reflection & Controversy	**Item 2332**	**$18.95**	_____
Social Work Speaks	Item 2340	$28.95	_____
Research on Children	Item 2235	$12.95	_____

+ 10% postage and handling _____

Total _____

☐ I've enclosed my check or money order for $ _____

☐ Please charge my   ☐ NASW Visa   ☐ Other Visa   ☐ MasterCard

  Credit Card No._____Exp. Date_____

  Signature _____

Name _____

Address _____

City_____State_____Zip_____

(Make checks payable to NASW Press.) Prices are subject to change.

NASW Distribution Center   Credit card orders call **1-800-227-3590**

P.O. Box 431   (In metro DC, call 301-317-8688)

Annapolis JCT, MD 20701   NASW PRESS   Or fax your order to **301-206-7989**

*RC 1/94